LIBRARY OF THE EARLY CIVILIZATIONS
EDITED BY PROFESSOR STUART PIGGOTT

Early Highland Peoples of ANATOLIA

EARLY HIGH

McGraw-Hill Book

LAND PEOPLES OF

ANATOLIA

Seton Lloyd

Company   New York

DESIGNED AND PRODUCED BY THAMES AND HUDSON

DS57
.L55

CONTENTS

GENERAL EDITOR'S PREFACE

The land mass of Asia Minor, thrusting westwards from the Levant and the Caucasus to the very quaysides of Constantinople, has throughout history and prehistory made a bridge between the east and west, and not for nothing did the Achaemenid kings build the Royal Road from Susa to Sardis. The phases of Anatolian prehistory and early history described in Professor Lloyd's volume include some very remarkable instances of the peculiarly international nature of the country and its civilizations in antiquity.

In the second half of the third millennium BC we encounter a series of spectacular finds best described as Royal Tombs and Treasures—tombs at Alaca Hüyük, Horoz Tepe and other sites in the Mahmatlar area; treasures there, in the second settlement of Troy and probably elsewhere in the Troad. Professor Lloyd includes here the now vanished objects allegedly from tombs at Dorak, but some of us would prefer to suspend judgement on these, since the numerous and extraordinary pieces cannot be regarded as a valid, closed find established under archaeological control. However, the finds from the other sites are dramatic enough, and the Alaca tombs, with their rich offerings in gold, silver, copper and iron are members of a type which Gordon Childe noted as a recurrent phenomenon in certain forms of social organization, with examples in the Royal Tombs at Ur, the princely graves of Shang China or the Mycenae Shaft Graves, the Scythian tombs or that of Sutton Hoo. With tombs go treasures – the interchange of gifts between princes is part of the code of the heroic aristocracies of the ancient world which also finds expression in the tombs; it is the Homeric *keimelion*, of gold, bronze or iron; silver or fine cloth. Each prince accumulated treasure and kept it secure, but the stock constantly changed as gifts were received and reciprocated, circulating among courts and citadels over a wide area, and for a long time.

The Alaca graves have their counterparts across the Black Sea in the Kuban, with Maikop or Novosvobodnaya in the later third millennium, or in the Caucasus rather later, as at Trialeti, Kirovakan or Lchashen, at the last site with hide burials in a manner common in South Russia and again present at Alaca. Contemporary with these later tombs are the Mycenae

Shaft Graves, structurally similar to Alaca, and types of gold-work and other ornaments are also shared throughout the wide Carpatho-Caspian province, where treasures range from Euboea and Poliochni on Lemnos, to later finds such as those of Perşinari in Rumania or at Borodino in Bessarabia, where fine stone battle-axes echo those of the Trojan treasure.

With the Hittites establishing themselves in Anatolia by the beginning of the second millennium BC, we are confronted with a people who, owing to their adoption of literacy through the cuneiform script, we know to have spoken languages within the Indo-European group. Their presence in Asia Minor, first attested in the Assyrian merchants' documents from Kültepe, constitutes our earliest surviving evidence for these languages, which of course include Sanskrit and Greek, Latin and Celtic, as well as the Slav group. The Hittites certainly reached the area in which they established their kingdom from outside, imposing themselves as overlords (as did the Aryans in India) on an already urban substrate culture. With the general archaeological and linguistic evidence pointing to South Russia as a likely original home of Indo-European speech, the connections between the cultures north of the Black Sea and Anatolia at the time of the Alaca Royal Tombs take on an added significance.

After the collapse of the main strongholds of Hittite power at the end of the second millennium BC, Professor Lloyd discusses the survival of a fragmented Hittite culture in the Anti-Taurus and North Syria, and the two successor-states of the Urartians of eastern Anatolia and beyond, and the Phrygians on the west. Both were peoples skilled in metallurgy: Urartian bronze vessels of high craftsmanship seem to have been traded westwards, probably to North Syrian ports, before the conquest of Urartu by Assyria in the middle-eighth century. Their great cauldrons especially inspired the manufacture of such vessels first in Greece, but within a couple of generations or so as far away to the north-west as the British Isles.

The Phrygians present many fascinating problems, some now being resolved by the Gordion excavations. Here we see the Phrygians in their eighth-century splendour – but when did their ancestors originally enter Anatolia, and whence? Assyrian records imply them to be in Asia Minor by the early eleventh century, and Greek tradition brought them from or through Thrace. The great tumulus burials with wooden mortuary houses described vividly in this book are in the manner of the Scyths and their ancestors on the Russian Steppe. Is prehistory repeating itself, and are we back in the same situation as that of the Alaca tombs?

STUART PIGGOTT

INTRODUCTION

To the composite work called *Dawn of Civilization* I contributed a chapter dealing with the early peoples and antiquities of Anatolia. In time, it was restricted to the so-called Bronze and Iron Ages, because the earlier Chalcolithic and Neolithic periods had already been effectively treated in another chapter. The style and content of the essay were primarily directed towards those who might be approaching the subject for the first time, but it was also intended to carry a quota of authentically reliable and up-to-date information. Apart from the restricted length of the first essay, which resulted in the rather cavalier treatment of certain subjects, six further years of intensive archaeological research have now taken place in Anatolia, culminating in the summer season of 1965, when more than fifty expeditions, either Turkish or foreign, contributed to our present total of archaeological information.

All this has made a reconsideration of the old text necessary, and the greater part of it has been re-written, in the hope of doing justice, not only to the actual finds which have been made in recent years, but to the stimulating interpretations with which scholarship has already illuminated them. And here one should make a cautionary reservation, to the effect that an attempt of this sort must depend for its success on the promptitude with which such discoveries are published. Preliminary reports are often long deferred: or they appear piecemeal as journal articles in a variety of languages. Where they are available, I have tried to assimilate and summarize them, but would wish to add that the task has been greatly facilitated by use of the admirable 'summary' which Machteld Mellink publishes annually in the *American Journal of Archaeology*. In another American journal, with acknowledgements to great scholars in the Anatolian field such as Kurt Bittel and Albrecht Goetze, the same author has presented us with one of those periodical assessments of trends and portents in archaeological interpretation, of which few are capable and to which many look forward. This, too, I have drawn on in the following pages.

It should perhaps be added that not all archaeological enterprises at present in progress obtain a mention in my review, even though they may already have continued for some years. This is because their results, as announced to date, have been too technical in character for their wider implications to be yet apparent. Among Turkish excavations in particular, there are cases where, available at the moment are only the raw materials from which important conclusions can be anticipated. Cases in point are Sedat Alp's stratigraphical sequence of Early Bronze Age settlements at Karahüyük-Konya; Nimet Ozgüç's work on the Middle Bronze Age city at Acemhüyük near Aksaray (a complementary operation to her husband's excavations at Kanesh); Bahadir Alkim's palace and tombs in the Tilmenhüyük-Gedikli mounds, and Kemal Balkan's Urartian finds at Patnos.

For the rest, it is hoped that the accounts of new discoveries included in these pages may serve to emphasize our improved understanding of Anatolian antiquity and of the part played by this miniature continent in the creation of Near Eastern civilization.

S.L.

CHAPTER ONE

The Early Metal Ages

Anatolia is a modern name applied to Asiatic Turkey; to the great peninsula of Asia Minor, thrust out from the main continent towards south-east Europe. The name is taken from the Turkish form, *Anadolu*, but at no time until the present had Asia Minor been thought of as a single political or geographical unit. The structure of the country is dominated by the great Anatolian Plateau, bounded on the north and south by mountain ridges severing it from the coastal plains, where climate and altitude combine to produce distinctively different territories. To the west the plateau descends more gently to the Aegean and the Sea of Marmara: to the east it merges gradually into the alpine landscape of Azerbaijan.

This geographical diversity is reflected in the prehistory and early recorded history of Anatolia, which shows no centralized or otherwise coherent pattern of development, such as one may observe in Egypt or Mesopotamia. One watches instead an assemblage of interdependent cultural enclaves, variously reacting upon each other, though effectively linked only by the great routes of passage for trade and migration which traverse the peninsula from end to end. Superficially, among early students of Anatolian antiquity, this picture created a tendency to belittle the probability that such a country could have made any independent contribution to the creation of Near Eastern civilization. Anatolia came to be seen by them only as a field for colonial activities or as a migratory transit-station between east and west. In the course of time, this view has come to be totally discarded, and it has on the contrary proved possible to establish the integrity of the country's corporate tradition and the autonomous character of its overall achievement. In fact, one of the most striking results of thirty years intensified research has been the discovery in Anatolia of a deep-seated aboriginal culture, productive of ideas and capable of transmitting them elsewhere.

Ill. 1

If we are now to substantiate this claim, we must first consider the successive phases which archaeologists have been able to detect in the evolution of indigenous societies and the influence upon them of contributory migrations. Later we shall find such conclusions supplemented by evidence from historical and philological sources and it will become possible to determine the actual sequence of events with increasing precision. For, like other regions of Western Asia, the story of Anatolia divides itself into two distinct periods; that which preceded the use of writing and that which followed. In the first, its reconstruction depends exclusively on the results of excavation, while in the second these are augmented by the testimony of written records. Anatolia comes comparatively late into the field of literacy, for our first written documents are contemporary with the Old Babylonian period in Mesopotamia; hardly earlier than the nineteenth century B C which is a thousand years after the invention of writing in Sumer and Egypt. It appears too, not as an indigenous development but as a remote extension of Mesopotamian culture itself, and as a result of the setting up of Assyrian trading colonies in the Assyrian Plateau. The earliest documents in Anatolia are in fact those written by Assyrian merchants in their commercial centre of Kanesh (modern Kültepe) in Cappadocia, in their own cuneiform script, which was adopted by the contemporary Anatolian rulers of the city for their own purposes. However, this early business correspondence – accounts, bills-of-lading or records of litigation – gives us little precise historical information, and true historical documents, with references to political and military events, do not appear until five hundred years later, when the Hittite kings, still using the cuneiform script as a vehicle for their own Indo-European language, record their achievements.

Ill. 41

Our knowledge of all that happened in Anatolia before this period accordingly depends exclusively on the results of archaeological research. During the past three decades this has fortunately been widely extended and successful. It has carried back the story of human endeavour in these parts at least a further five thousand years and has introduced us to peoples who would otherwise have remained completely unknown to us. But, as people, they do remain without exception anonymous; so that, in discussing the sequence of developments in these early periods, we are compelled to fall back on the rather arbitrary terminology by which archaeology identifies the chronological epochs to which they belong. Here in Anatolia as elsewhere, the 'Neolithic Revolution' is separated from the beginning of the Bronze Age proper by a 'Chalcolithic' period. The Bronze Age is divided into the 'Early', 'Middle' and 'Late' phases, the first occupying in time the greater part of the third millennium BC, the second covering the period of the Assyrian colonies in the first half of the second millennium and the third corresponding to the centuries illuminated by the Hittite records, which ended with the destruction of the Hittite Empire in about 1200 BC.

The clear historical character of this later period, the evidence of political development and religious thought,

Comparative stratigraphy table:

DATES	PERIOD	NORTHWEST		CENTRAL				SOUTH-WEST	SOUTH		EAST	
612				(SARDIS) ←— L Y D I A N S —→					CARCHEMISH SINJERLI		KARMIR BLUR ALTINTEPE	
		←——— P H R Y G I A N S ———→							NEO-HITTITES		U R A R T U	
900		MONUMENTS GORDION		TOWN		TOWN			MALATYA		TOPRAKKALE PATNOS KAYALIDERE	
		TROY	TROAD & ISLANDS	KÜLTEPE	ALISHAR	ALACA	BOGHAZ-KÖY	BEYCE-SULTAN	TARSUS	KARA-HÜYÜK-KONYA	KARAZ	MALATYA
1200	LATE BRONZE	VII A					HITTITE EMPIRE	↑ I / SMALL PRINCIPALITY II				
1700							HITTITE OLD KINGDOM	III				
	MIDDLE BRONZE			LEVEL IA		3B		SQUATTERS	M.B. IV			
1750				LEVEL IB ③ KARUM TABLETS			KARUM TABLETS	IV	M.B. III	↑ I		
1825		VI		LEVEL II ② KARUM TABLETS	II	4						
1850								V	M.B. II			
1900				①				BURNT PALACE				
1950					III	5			M.B. I	↓ III		
	EARLY BRONZE ③	V		LEVELS III & IV ⓐ PRE-ASSYRIAN KARUM				VII & VI	E.B IIIb	↑ IV		E.B IIIb
		IV		ⓑ MEGARON 'TEMPLE'		6		X - VIII				E.B IIIa
		III		ALABASTER 'IDOLS' ⓒ				XII & XI	E.B IIIa			
2300						PONTIC CEMETERIES				↓ VI		
	EARLY BRONZE ②	II	DORAK YORTAN			ROYAL TOMBS 7		XVIII-XIII	E.B II	VII	E.B II	
2500					IB							
	EARLY BRONZE ①	I	YORTAN			8		XIX-XVII	E.B I		E.B I	
3000			THERMI POLYOCHNI KUMTEPE			9						

(CENTRAL columns are annotated vertically: "ANITTA" and "CAPPADOCIAN" for the Middle Bronze levels; "LATE CAPPADOCIAN" and "EARLY CAPPADOCIAN" for the Early Bronze levels.)

1 A diagram showing the comparative stratigraphy of excavations at Bronze and Iron Age sites in Anatolia. The evidence of written records begins to be available in the nineteenth century BC

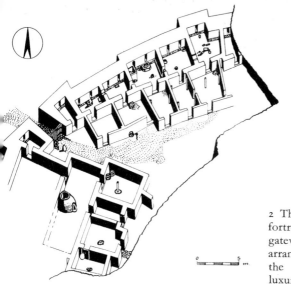

2 The excavated area of a small prehistoric fortress at Mersin in Cilicia. The towered gateway is flanked on one side by neatly arranged quarters for the garrison, and on the other by the commander's more luxurious residence

the sequence of royal names and the battles or treaties associated with them, all serve to emphasize the contrasting impersonality of the 'archaeological' age which preceded it. One cannot however fail to be impressed by the astonishing detail of the anthropological picture which it has proved possible to reconstruct, simply through the patient and meticulous study of its material remains. It should be mentioned at this point that, for the purpose of this study, it may be necessary to assume some previous knowledge of the earliest chapters in the archaeological story, the Neolithic and Chalcolithic phases having been dealt with in a previous volume of the series. There, against a background of painstakingly recorded stratigraphy, distribution or typology and the cautious inferences to be made from them, we have seen some of the great highlights of recent discovery, when some aspect of life in a prehistoric community was suddenly and brilliantly illuminated by chance or through the peculiar ingenuity of an excavator.

Examples which come easily to mind are the Neolithic township at Çatal Hüyük, a Chalcolithic village at Hacılar and the miniature fortress at Mersin dating from the early fourth millennium B C. All these are to be considered retrospectively if the theme of continuity in the evolution

Ill. 2

of essentially 'Anatolian' culture is to be traced to its primitive beginnings. Meanwhile, for our present purpose the thread must be taken up at the opening of the Bronze Age in approximately 3000 B C.

The Anatolian Early Bronze Age

Ill. 3

Already, at the beginning of the third millennium B C one finds the country divided into six or seven fairly well-defined provinces, distinguished by slight disparities in their archaeological remains; and it is, as we have said, in no way surprising that the form and disposal of these is largely dictated by geography. The comparative study of contemporary developments in them has been made possible by the excavation in each of at least one well-stratified ancient site. Thus, there is a north-west province which includes the site of Troy, where excavations have resulted in the determination of an exemplary archaeological sequence. Next, a large part of the plateau proper, including the famous Halys Bend, falls within what has come to be called the Central Anatolian province, and here too the Early Bronze Age is admirably documented by Turkish excavations at Alaca Hüyük and Kültepe, the Middle Bronze Age also by Kültepe and the Late Bronze Age by excavations at the Hittite capital, Hattušaš (Boghazköy). Eastern Anatolia has an archaeological character of its own, less well known, but typified by finds at Karaz, near Erzerum. There is an extensive south-western province, whose Bronze Age history has been revealed at Beycesultan, and a Cilician province dependent on sequences discovered at Tarsus and Mersin. Finally there are minor provinces such as that covering the area watered by the Sangarius (Sakarya) river and named after the site called Demirci Hüyük, a Pontic province to the north of the Halys area, and the Konya Plain about which more is known in earlier periods. The combined results of studies at all these sites have recently

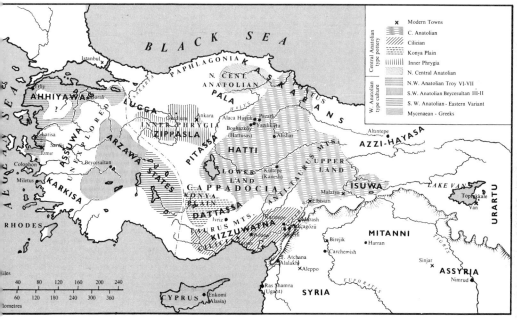

3 A map of Anatolia showing the ancient sites which have been excavated. The central plateau, mountain ranges and coastal plains determine the country's provincial divisions during the Bronze Age

made it possible for archaeologists to sub-divide the Early Bronze Age into three sub-phases, numbered from the earliest upwards and it may perhaps here be convenient to summarize the recorded developments during each of these in turn.

The first phase, known as Early Bronze I, is everywhere less well documented than those which succeeded it. No royal tombs, temples or palaces have yet been found to suggest the quality of luxury goods in circulation among the privileged classes, or the trend in religious thought and political organization. Already, however, there is evidence to justify the distinction which has been made between this period and the Chalcolithic Age which preceded it. In its name, the word 'bronze' is in fact no more than a categorical convenience, since the bulk of the metal now used is copper, and the toughening of copper by an admixture of tin was as yet only properly understood in the maritime trading centres with their more sophisticated knowledge of metallurgy. Nevertheless simple forms of metal objects are now fairly plentiful and, judging from the frequency with which metallic shapes are simulated in the designs of pottery, the coppersmith's craft may already have reached a fairly high standard. The exploitation of Anatolia's mineral wealth which now began, created, by the end of the Bronze Age, a source of supply to the principal countries of the Near East. At Troy this period is represented by the first settlement founded on virgin rock. It is a small fortress, hardly more than a hundred yards in diameter, but it was the first site to provide reliable criteria – pottery shapes and small objects – of the Early Bronze I culture. This extended beyond the Anatolian mainland to off-shore islands such as Lemnos (Poliochni) and Lesbos (Thermi) where archaeological characteristics of the era are perhaps even better illustrated than at Troy itself. They include the first instances of dwelling-houses built to the so-called 'megaron' plan: a rectangular hall with central hearth and an open porch at one end; a device which two-and-a-half millennia later dictated the form of a Greek temple. In western Anatolia at this time the dead were buried in extra-mural cemeteries often in large clay 'pithos' vessels.

Ill. 4

Many of these have been brought to light by illicit excavation at Yortan in the Troad, but the grave goods are poor and no corresponding settlements have yet been firmly associated with them.

Troy I was burnt and destroyed in some disaster, and cultural changes in the more impressive citadel which replaced it initiate a second phase of the Early Bronze Age. Now at last we are afforded a more revealing panorama of contemporary life; a picture of native

4 A 'face' urn and other Early Bronze Age pottery from graves at Yortan in the Troad. These correspond in time with the earliest fortress at Troy and with comparable settlements in offshore islands such as Lemnos and Lesbos

dynasties controlling the various Anatolian provinces, profiting from an advanced metal industry based on local production centres, actively trading among themselves and accumulating evidence of material wealth in their fortresses and metropolitan centres. Troy II itself makes its own contribution to this picture by its architecture and by the hoards of jewellery and other luxury objects, found by Schliemann buried beneath its palace and christened by him 'Priam's Treasure'. Elsewhere in the Troad from a group of Royal tombs (to whose discovery some mystery attaches), we have the so-called 'Dorak Treasure', testifying to an even higher standard of craftsmanship and a wider variety of precious materials. Finds of this sort are no longer restricted to the north-west province. Tarsus in Cilicia has another prosperous maritime culture and, above all, central Anatolia comes into its own with

Ills. 26–28

Ills. 19–25

an inland counterpart of these coastal dynasties, showing a striking concentration of power and wealth. Here again it is from a group of ceremonial burials – the now-famous Royal Tombs at Alaca Hüyük – that our knowledge is obtained, and their contents have been supplemented by similar burials, more recently discovered at Horoztepe and Mahmatlar in the Pontic province. At Beycesultan too, the type-site of the south-western province, there are religious shrines with valuable evidence of ritual and an important record of ceramic criteria among their votive deposits. The finds in these inland provinces suggest an intensive exchange of goods and traditions, dependent here upon the great caravan routes, just as in the coastal areas they are correspondingly facilitated by shipping. Tombs and places of worship now add their quota of religious and iconographic information. We may now examine some of these finds in greater detail.

Alaca Hüyük

Excavating in the deeper levels of the Hittite city-mound at Alaca Hüyük, Turkish archaeologists discovered a group of thirteen tombs, perhaps those of a local ruling family in the Early Bronze II phase, buried among the paraphernalia of funerary ritual and accompanied by their private possessions. The interments had evidently been made at long intervals, over several generations. Some were single tombs; others contained the remains of both a man and a woman buried on different occasions, which suggests that when the first interment was made the location of the tomb must have been marked on the surface. *Ill. 10* Men were accompanied by their weapons, women by their ornaments or toilet articles, and both by domestic *Ill. 9* vessels and utensils mostly of precious metals. Notable among the weapons was a dagger with a crescent-shaped handle and a blade of iron – a metal known to have been many times more valuable than gold at this time – and

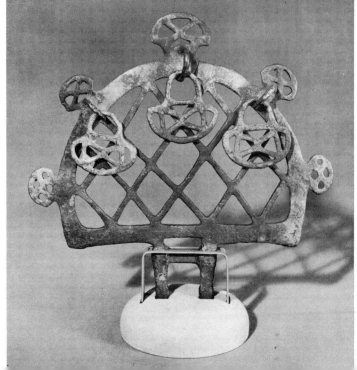

5, 6 Bronze ornaments from the Royal tombs at Alaca Hüyük, called 'standards' for want of a better name. In the group of free-standing animals (*above*) special significance seems to be attributed to the stag, which would suggest the mentality of a mountain people. The design (*below*) of an open-work grill with pendant ornaments is less comprehensible, though it has been identified by some as a sun symbol

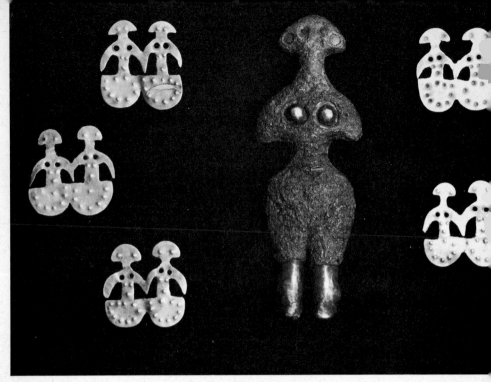

7 From a Royal tomb at Alaca, a large copper figurine having boots and breasts overlaid with gold. With it and stylistically comparable are appliqué ornaments of gold, representing paired figurines of the 'violin' type associated in the Bronze Age with a mother-goddess cult

Ills. 12–14   among the personal ornaments, a gold filigree diadem with a tassel of gold ribbon. Then there was a wide variety of objects connected with the funerary ritual –

Ills. 5, 6   strange open-work grills of bronze, sometimes adorned with animals. These have been called 'standards' because they were probably mounted at the head of a pole, and

Ill. 8   ornaments featuring similar animals, finely wrought in bronze and inlaid with silver, may have served the same

Ill. 7   purpose. There were also strange metal figurines, one of which was of bronze with boots and breasts enriched with gold. The tombs themselves were rectangular pits sometimes up to eighteen or twenty feet long and ten feet wide.

8 A bronze 'terminal' figure of a stag, its legs drawn together to fit ▷ the narrow base, attachable perhaps to a ceremonial staff or the upright element of a canopy. The inlaid ornament is of silver

9 From a tomb at Alaca Hüyük, a jug of gold with a very finely wrought *repoussé* ornament. Less pretentious vessels of this shape are found among the pottery of the period, sometimes ornamented, with fluting or incisions

Ill. 10

Ill. 11

They were lined with rough stone walling and covered in with a ceiling of wooden beams. Laid upon this were the skulls and hooves of cattle, which had evidently remained attached to the hides, the actual carcases having formed part of a funerary feast. The area covered by most of these tombs seemed far greater than was necessary to accommodate the bodies and surviving grave-goods which were grouped with wide spaces between. It was therefore assumed that these had been filled with other items of perishable materials, including wooden furniture. This was confirmed by discoveries subsequently made in the two Pontic cemeteries which we have already mentioned.

The Pontic Tombs

The tombs at Horoztepe and Mahmatlar, both of which are in the neighbourhood of Tokat to the north-east of Alaca Hüyük, provide an important supplement to those at Alaca itself. The typology and associations of objects from the three sources are most interesting when studied collectively. Unfortunately, at the two Pontic sites less could be learnt about the form and lay-out of the graves, owing to the circumstances of their discovery. In both cases this resulted from chance finds by peasants and in that of Horoztepe much damage had been done by the intrusion of a modern graveyard. Nevertheless, from the latter at least, a great wealth of material has been recovered through careful archaeological treatment. The tombs, which approximated in size to those of Alaca Hüyük, were not in this case lined with stone walls. There was no trace of a timber covering or of animal bones overlying them. The metal grave goods, which appeared to have been deliberately bent or folded in order to occupy less space, were piled untidily at the feet of the skeletons, few remains of which survived. As we have said, various forms of furniture were prominent, including two tables, one rectangular and one oval, with four legs ending in boot-shaped feet, all constructed of bronze. There were also a wide variety of attachments in bronze for other types of wooden furniture. Other objects are without parallel at Alaca Hüyük; a grotesque figure in bronze of a mother nursing a child, eight inches high; *Ill. 15* sistrums (rattles) decorated with animal figures and new *Ill. 17* varieties of terminal ornaments in animal form. Small *Ill. 18* objects only were of gold or silver. The remainder, of bronze, included many household vessels; fruit-stands, beak-spouted pitchers, basket-handled teapots, jars, bowls, platters and cups as well as a number of weapons. *Ill. 16* The stylistic evidence of all these objects has now been very carefully studied and it has been concluded that

10, 11 Artist's reconstructions of a Royal tomb at Alaca Hüyük. *Above*, the king lies upon a bier, awaiting burial in a walled tomb in which the queen is already buried with her possessions and ornaments. *Left*, the timber construction of the roof is shown and upon it, heads and horns still attached to the skins of animals sacrificed for the funeral feast

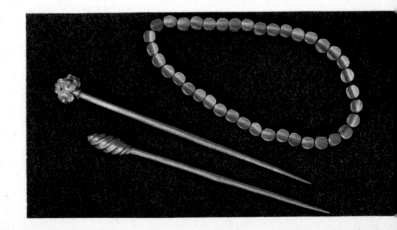

12–14 Jewellery, gold vessels, ornaments and weapons from the Royal tombs. *Above*, a gold jug and a drinking-cup ornamented in *repoussé*, a bronze 'standard' of the open grille variety, a gold buckle and pin with other ornaments (*also below left*). *Below*, a gold diadem with ribbon and a gold bracelet, both in filigree work with a gold-mounted marble mace between. In the metal-smith's work of the period, few processes were unknown

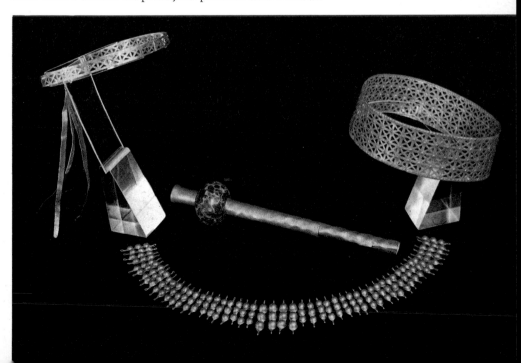

15, 16 Metal objects from rich cemeteries in the Pontic region some hundreds of miles north of Alaca Hüyük. A grotesque female figure in bronze (*left*) carries a child at her breast. Weapons (*above*) include several forms of battle-axe. Unlike the Alaca tombs, these contained few objects of gold or silver and are dated slightly later; *c* 2100 BC

those from Horoztepe show conclusively signs of technical development a little in advance of those from Alaca. In fact their excavators have concluded that they must be contemporary with or a little in advance of the latest burial at Alaca, perhaps more properly belonging to the third Early Bronze phase, for they are inclined to date them to approximately 2100 BC while the burials at Alaca Hüyük may have started a good deal earlier. By other forms of reasoning it has also been suggested that techniques and practices evident in the Horoztepe cemetery indicate a culture indigenous to the Pontic province, and that the rulers buried at Alaca represent the temporary intrusion into Central Anatolia of an alien aristocracy from that source. Apart from this, other conclusions are made possible by the combined inventories of these tombs. The figures of deer and bulls, evidently sacred

Ill. 18

17, 18 Bronze objects from the tombs at Horoztepe in Pontus; a sistrum or ceremonial rattle (*left*) decorated with carnivorous as well as ruminant animals, and (*right*) the 'terminal' figure of a bull. Pontus is thought to be the original home of the Alaca Hüyük culture

emblems too, are notably un-Mesopotamian in style and subject. The technique too, by which bronze is enriched with more precious metals and coloured stones, appears to be characteristically Anatolian and both prefigure subsequent developments in the art of Hittite times.

Dorak and 'Priam's Treasure'

In striking contrast to these northern tombs are those reported from Dorak, by which the character and wealth of the north-western province at the same period were so dramatically revealed. On a small rock promontory, overlooking Lake Apolyont, near Bursa, a large cist-grave measuring ten feet by six contained the body of a local ruler and his wife: a smaller one had a single male burial and nearby 'pithos' burials were perhaps those of servants. The men had been buried with their weapons and

Ills. 24, 25

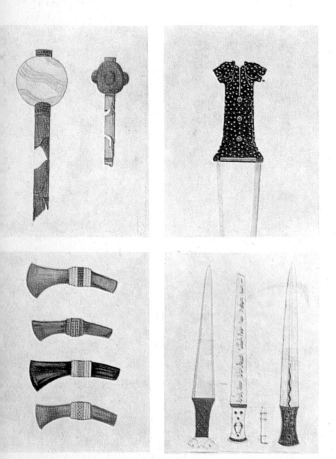

19-22 A 'treasure' of objects, mostly in precious metals and semi-precious stones, said to be derived from tombs discovered at Dorak in the eastern Troad, though the elaborately wrought figurines (*above*) may have a different provenance. In addition to vessels (*opposite above*) and weapons (*left*) of silver and gold, the rare materials used include amber, turquoise, ivory and rock-crystal, as well as iron, which was then more valuable than gold. Also, sufficiently preserved to retain the colouring was the remnant of a woven floor-covering (*opposite below*). Etched upon the blade of one silver dagger (*left, below centre*) were drawings of sailing-ships and a dolphin. The treasure is thought to be contemporary with settlement IIg at Troy; *c.*2300 BC

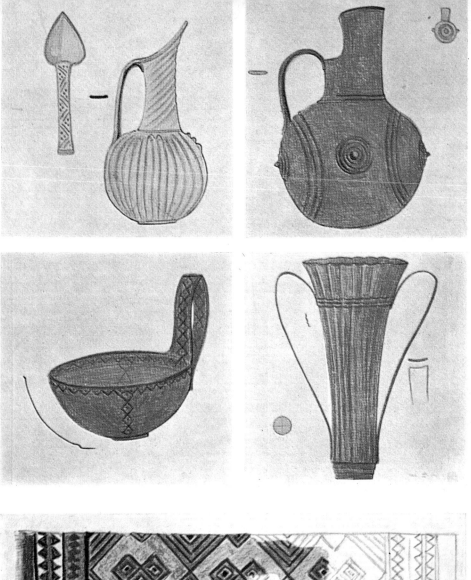

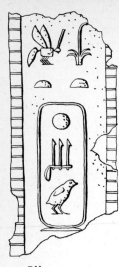

the woman with her ornaments and personal belongings. One man had the bones of his dog with him and, possibly derived from some other source, there were female figurines, perhaps of the 'dancing-girl' or 'concubine' type, whose dress and appearance are meticulously reproduced in precious materials. The tombs are dated, not only by domestic vessels of gold and silver but, almost miraculously, by a fragment of gold overlay from a wooden throne, bearing an inscription in Egyptian hieroglyphs which includes the name of Sahure, the second king of the Fifth Dynasty of Old Kingdom Egypt. Finally there were the remains of a woven floor-covering in which both the pattern and the colours of the thread are still distinguishable. The objects in these graves are from several points of view completely distinctive. The materials themselves are varied and rare enough to suggest far-reaching trade facilities – amber for instance, and turquoise, ivory and rock-crystal as well as iron – but the modelling of organic and other forms is almost Egyptian in its elegance. The figurines are of interest, not only because they reveal a minor aspect of contemporary dress, but because the highest form of craftsmanship is applied to them as it also is applied to other profane objects, such as weapons and domestic vessels. At Alaca it is reserved for objects with religious purposes. Among the Dorak finds there are other indications of reaction to environment. Not far from the site today, fishing boats pass and dolphins play among the waters of the Marmara. And here at Dorak are Early Bronze Age ships engraved on the blade of a dagger while its point is decorated with the shape of a dolphin. The Aegean background has replaced the forests of north Anatolia.

The repertory of Early Bronze Age luxury goods in north-west Anatolia is greatly enriched, particularly where jewellery is concerned, by the 'treasures' dating from the final occupation of the Second Settlement at

Ill. 23
Ill. 22

Ill. 19

Ill. 20

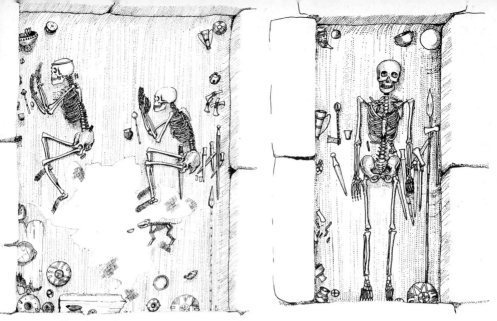

24, 25 Sketches of two cist graves at Dorak purporting to show the positions in which the tomb-furniture was found. The male figurine in the larger grave on the left is accompanied by the skeleton of his dog. The graves appear to be lined with dressed stone

Troy. With records of all these finds available, one obtains a clear view of the materials obtainable by trade, and the techniques already devised for shaping and using them. Among the metals are copper, iron, gold, silver, electrum and lead, while bronze was occasionally made with imported tin. Metal was treated by casting in closed moulds or *cire perdue*, hammering or *repoussé* work, sweating or soldering. Ornament was contrived by granulation, filigree or *cloisonné* inlay. Semi-precious stones and other ornamental materials included carnelian, jasper, nephrite, obsidian, meerschaum, and locally made faience, in addition to those already mentioned individually. Some of them were used in making ceremonial models of contemporary weapons, of which the most varied collection comes from Troy IIg. There are battle-axes, rock-crystal and lion-headed pommels for swords and daggers, and dagger-blades of silver as well as bronze. There is also evidence to suggest that shields and helmets were used, though these have not yet been found.

Ills. 26–28

Ill. 20

33

26–28 Gold ornaments found by Schliemann beneath the palace in the second settlement at Troy (*c.* 2300 BC) and christened by him 'Priam's Treasure'. *Above* is a steel engraving of Mrs Schliemann wearing some of the jewellery. *Below*, a filigree bracelet and smaller ornaments with designs based on the double spiral, a motif which appears throughout the Near East at this period

29, 30 The ruins of Troy (*above*), as they are seen today. *Right* is a reconstructed plan of Settlement IIg; a walled fortress with a single, heavily fortified entrance gate. In the centre is the great 'megaron' assembly-hall and to the west the residential palace. Area: about five acres

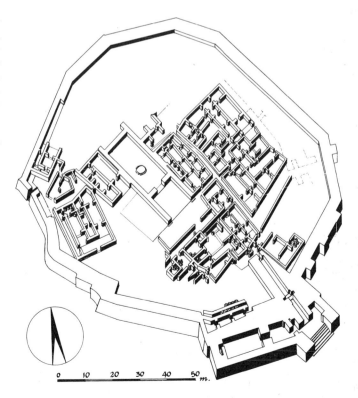

0   10   20   30   40   50
m.

Architecture

Ill. 30

It is also to the fortress of Level IIg at Troy that one turns for enlightenment on the architectural appearance and lay-out of an Early Bronze city. The vast 'megaron' hall, occupying a central enclosure and standing among the network of more normal sized buildings that surround it, had a roof-span of thirty feet and can easily be recognized for what it is – the main public building or assembly-hall of the community. The actual residential quarters of the ruling family can also probably be identified in a complex of less pretentious buildings to the west of it. The city-walls with their great towered gateway, constructed of mud brick in a timber framework on a sub-structure of dressed stone, seem almost disproportionately substantial in relation to the buildings which they enclose. The private houses seem to have been lightly built of brick on stone foundations and to have had fragile upper storeys of plaster in a framework of wood. Closely clustered together over narrow alley-ways, they must have

Ill. 29

resembled the half-timber slums of Jacobean London. When the Second Settlement was destroyed by fire it must have burnt as easily; everywhere Schliemann found fallen walls, their mud bricks baked into solid masses among the calcined rubble of their stone foundations.

There is nothing recognizable as a temple in Troy II. For some rare examples of religious buildings one must turn to Beycesultan in the south-western province, where

Ill. 33

they took the form of rectangular shrine-chambers arranged in pairs (perhaps because they were dedicated to separate male and female deities). Each had an 'altar', surrounded by *ex voto* objects and consisting of twin *stelae* between which the offerings were passed over a built-in structure resembling the 'horns of consecration' in Minoan buildings of a later age. A feature also of the

Ills. 31, 32

'male' shrine was an isolated wooden post reminiscent of the 'tree' or 'pillar' cults of Crete.

31–33 At Beycesultan on the Upper Meander Early Bronze Age shrines are arranged in pairs, perhaps with a dual dedication. In the centre is a complex altar (*above*) consisting of twin stelae and 'horns of consecration'. *Below* a similar shrine is reconstructed with its free-standing wooden 'pillar'. In both cases votive pottery is abundant and a portion of the chamber behind the altar is screened off. Religious buildings of the Early Bronze Age are rare in Anatolia

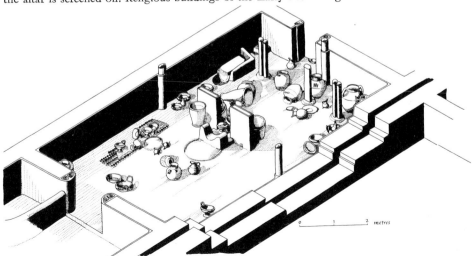

CHAPTER TWO

Kültepe in the Early and Middle Bronze Ages

The Early Bronze Age

The final centuries of the third millennium B C seem to have been a time of major migrations. One of these occurred at the beginning of the third Early Bronze phase. In about 2300 B C a great wave of Indo-European peoples, speaking a dialect known as Luvian, seems to have swept over Anatolia from the direction of the Bosphorus, occupying practically the whole south-western part of the country up to a diagonal line drawn approximately from the Marmara to the Gulf of Iskanderun. Their progress was marked by signs of widespread destruction and for about a century, at sites where remains of this period have been found, there is every indication of a decline in prosperity. The northern and central provinces, however, remained unaffected and, in about 2200 B C when contact with the Luvian-dominated south-west had been re-established, they found themselves able and ready to resume profitable trade-contacts particularly with Cilicia and the north Syrian markets beyond. Under these circumstances the focus of attention moves once more to Central Anatolia and particularly to the site of Kültepe (Kanesh) which will presently, at the beginning of the Middle Bronze Age, be illuminated by the advent of literate Assyrian colonists. The merchants were to reside in a suburb of their own at the foot of the mound, but excavations of the pre-Assyrian levels on the mound itself have begun to reveal the historical prelude to their arrival played out by indigenous peoples during the closing phase of the Early Bronze Age.

This period is of special interest, and its stratigraphy worth sorting out from the information so far available in preliminary reports. It is the period of the so-called 'Cappadocian' painted pottery whose significance has tended in the past to become extremely controversial. First discovered by the American excavators of Alishar and misleadingly labelled by them 'Alishar III' owing to a stratigraphical misunderstanding, this brightly ornamental pottery with designs in several colours appeared to them and others to be an exotic intrusion among the drab burnished wares which were the rule elsewhere. By some it had even been associated with the arrival of the Hittites, an Indo-European people who, like the Luvians, began to make their appearance in Anatolia at the end of the Early Bronze Age. This theory has now been discarded by the excavator of Kültepe, who sees it, not as an importation from elsewhere but as a local development, peculiar to the Cappadocian area evolved during the Early Bronze III stage from monochrome wares with simpler designs (Alishar 'Intermediate'). In following its evolution he has been able to distinguish three successive sub-phases each of them marked by important architectural and other developments on the Kültepe mound. Perhaps the most important of these belongs to the second sub-phase. It is a large building, now thought to be a temple, which is built on the 'megaron' principle; a square hall entered axially through an open porch, with minor rooms annexed on both sides. The hall, which is covered with white plaster, has a huge circular hearth in the centre, surrounded by four wooden columns, and the portico has low 'sleeping-platforms' on each side. There

Ill. 1

Ill. 34

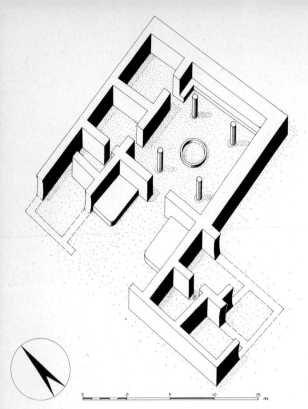

34 A building, now thought to be a temple, of the 'megaron' type found on the main mound at Kültepe and dating from a final phase of the Early Bronze Age (*c.*2100 BC). The square hall with 4 columns, central hearth and open portico with 'sleeping-platforms' are all features to be found in Mycenaean palaces almost a thousand years later

are parallels to this building in exactly the same period at Beycesultan Level VIII, but the close resemblance of this example to the Mycenaean palaces of a thousand years later is most striking. Another unique feature, appearing in both the first and the second sub-phase of this 'Cappadocian' period at Kültepe, is a class of alabaster figurines, unique in Anatolia. Of two types represented, one appears *Ill. 35* to be a seated goddess: the other is more abstract and *Ill. 36* consists of a disc-like body with one or more projecting heads, pig-tailed and wearing conical head-dresses. Others again hold children and quite complicated groups are attempted. Some of these idols were found in a new type of grave; a circular stone tomb with two compartments, one for the body and the other for votive offerings. Associated both with graves and buildings throughout are forms of pottery and small objects which again suggest a close trade connection with Cilicia, Syria and, in

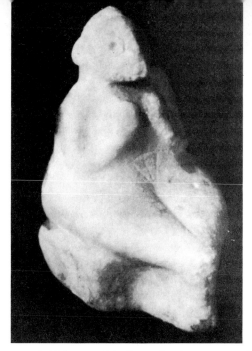

35, 36 Alabaster idols from circular stone tombs a little older than the Early Bronze Age 'megaron' at Kültepe. One type often represents a seated goddess (*left*). Others (*right*) are more ideoplastic symbols with decorated, disc-like bodies and projecting heads

the case of certain small gold ornaments, even with Mesopotamia. Pottery shapes include well-known features such as the goblet with two high handles, called by Schliemann the 'depas amphikypellon' and the so-called 'red-cross bowl', which would be equally at home at this time at Troy or in south-western Anatolia, as well as 'Syrian bottles' and a variety of typical Cilician forms.

Here then at Kültepe, these final centuries of the Early Bronze Age are beginning to be well documented. And it is to the same site that we shall primarily turn to watch the introduction of a literate culture in the Middle Bronze. Before doing so, however, we should note an independent development which has been taking place in eastern Anatolia. Here, among the high altitudes of modern Turkey's eastern province, sites like Karaz, near Erzerum, show, as might perhaps be expected, Early Bronze cultures more obviously connected with Azerbaijan and

even with the steppe region north of the Caucasus. At
Trialeti, near Tiflis, tumulus burials have been found
whose contents include East Anatolian black burnished
pottery, and, as burial mounds suggest a migrant people,
this has been associated with the movement which
brought Indo-Europeans to Anatolia. The discovery of
East Anatolian types among metal vessels as far afield as
the famous royal tomb at Maikop on the Kuban could
have the same implication.

The Middle Bronze Age

The first century of the second millennium BC saw great
changes in the cities of Anatolia and a new era of cultural
progress and prosperity began. The city of Kanesh had
grown too big to be accommodated on the summit of its

Ill. 38

ancient mound, and at its foot a new suburb was laid
out and surrounded by a wall almost two-thirds of a mile
long, making the total area of the town about 125 acres.
It is unknown whether in its early stages this suburb was
used exclusively by a commercial population, but after
its third rebuilding (Level II), it became the home of an
Assyrian merchant colony (*karum*). The expanding Assyrian kingdom, with its capital at Ashur, on the Tigris,
had taken control of the trade-route which brought metal
ores and other Anatolian products to Mesopotamia, and
had established half-a-dozen or more of such trading
posts in the most productive areas, of which Kanesh was
the most important. The status of these colonies in relation to the indigenous principalities has to be inferred
from the few relevant texts which have survived. There
is, unfortunately, no unanimous agreement among lingu-
ists as to the exact meaning of these but the majority are
satisfied that they existed by mutual agreement rather
than vassalage. The *karum* seems in any case to have
resembled a 'chamber-of-commerce' through the authority of which prices could be fixed, debts settled and

37 A fine vessel with polychrome ornament in the 'Cappadocian' style from Kültepe. These painted wares (once wrongly associated with the arrival of the Hittites), appeared first in the final phases of the Early Bronze Age and lasted until the Assyrian occupation in Level II of the *karum*, the period of the famous Kültepe tablets

38 The main mound at Kültepe (Kanesh) representing a walled city of the indigenous princes. Meadows in the foreground are the site of the suburb where the Assyrian merchants created a *karum* or commercial settlement. Here they conducted their business, and lived on friendly terms with their neighbours in the Anatolian city

transport arranged. Goods exported from Assyria included cloths and fabrics of widely varying qualities – some of them very costly – which were exchanged against copper and other minerals including carnelian, amber and a little iron, which at that time commanded five times the price of gold. Silver was used only as a form of currency. The goods were carried by the then-famous black donkeys of Cappadocia in caravans. These were led or organized by men called 'transport factors', who took responsibility for the delivery of goods and payments. They were often accompanied by official messengers carrying the equivalent of 'royal mail'. Something is known of the route they took, which passed by Sinjar to the crossroads city of Harran, then followed the 'Royal Road' of later times, crossing the Euphrates at Birejik and mounting to the Plateau by way of Marash and Elbistan. No case is recorded in the tablets of a caravan being interfered with on the way.

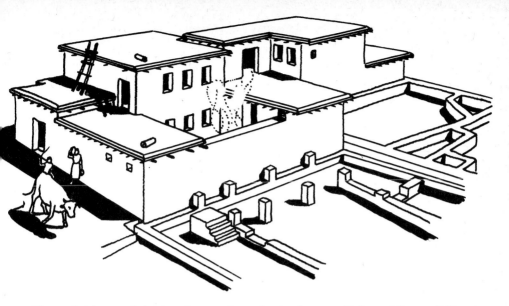

39 Flat-roofed house of the Assyrian merchants in the *karum* at Kültepe. Like small 'firms', each family conducted its business in the ground-floor rooms, keeping its records in cuneiform script on clay tablets which were afterwards baked in tall ovens. They lived on the floor above and made much use of the flat roof on summer evenings. They buried their dead beneath the floors of their houses with certain of their possessions. Among these are objects reminiscent of their native Assyria

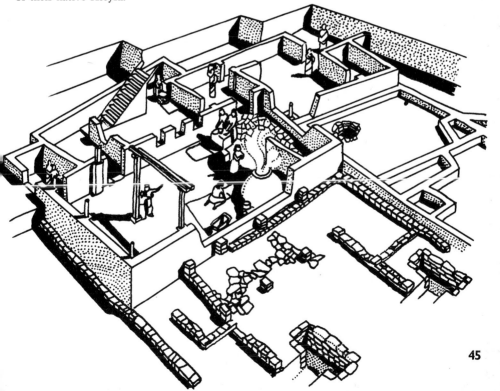

40 Reconstruction of the entrance to the Assyrian *karum* at Kültepe, a walled suburb almost one-third of a mile long. A caravan of the famous black donkeys of Cappadocia is entering the *karum* after checking in at the Anatolian city above, and paying dues to the ruling prince. The building on the right is perhaps the headquarters of the Assyrian mercantile organization where caravans unload. This institution served the secondary purpose of a tribunal for the fixing of prices and the settlement of disputes. It could arrange for the deposit of securities against a loan, or consider a creditor's claims against a debtor's capacity to pay. In the picture merchants are going about their business and scribes keeping their records on clay tablets which are subsequently baked. In the remote distance is the extinct volcano, Mount Argaeus, which overshadows modern Kayseri. The direction of the old trade-route from Kayseri to Ashur in Mesopotamia is approximately known

41 Cuneiform tablets from Kültepe, wrapped in clay envelopes, labelled and bearing the impression of a cylinder-seal. In the houses of the *karum* these were arranged on wooden shelves or stored in large earthenware vessels, labelled for identification

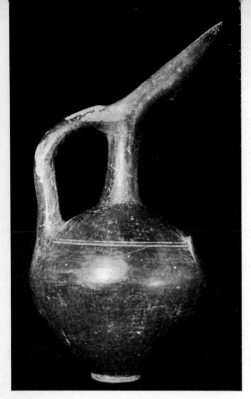

42, 43 Gracefully shaped pottery used at Kültepe in the time of the Assyrian merchants. These vessels are usually covered with a cream or bright red 'slip' and highly polished. Before the excavations at Kültepe they were known by the term 'Alishar II'

Ill. 40

Ill. 39

The merchants in their suburb seem to have lived on excellent terms with their Anatolian neighbours, and there was frequent intermarriage. Every consignment of goods, before delivery to the *karum*, had to pass through the 'palace' of the native ruler in the Anatolian city above, which exercised an option to buy and otherwise levied taxes. But this was done in an equitable and orderly manner and the colonists were otherwise left unmolested to practise their own customs. They seem for instance to have buried their dead beneath their houses, and these graves have been most fruitful of works of art, some of them of Mesopotamian character. The houses themselves on the other hand followed the old Anatolian tradition; a half-timber construction on a stone foundation. Certain rooms on the ground floor were used for storing tablets and the whole business archive of a merchant family has sometimes been recovered from a single house. When the tablets were found in place, they were generally neatly

44, 45 Houses at Kültepe were built on a characteristically Anatolian principle with brick walls on stone foundation, reinforced with timber beams and vertical posts. Rooms serving as kitchens (*right*) had horse-shoe-shaped hearths to support cooking-pots, large baking-ovens, braziers, water-coolers, storage-jars and a variety of smaller vessels, among which the brightly painted 'Cappadocian' ware (*above*) provided a touch of colour. The merchants intermarried with the Anatolian natives; so their domestic life conformed to local customs

46, 47 The potters of Kültepe showed an aptitude for modelling pottery in fantastic animal forms. Even vessels used for more practical purposes were sometimes adorned with small clay beasts or birds. The ritual 'pouring-vases' seen here represent the two current techniques in ornament; (*above*) the highly polished monochrome finish and (*below*) the polychrome painted decoration of 'Cappadocian' ware

48 A steatite mould from which clay plaques were probably made representing a 'holy family' of Anatolian deities

stacked on wooden shelves or stored in earthenware vessels, and their clay envelopes were often found intact, bearing the impression of the merchant's seal. Other rooms on the ground floor were kitchens or domestic offices, and here in orderly arrangement were found the beautiful pottery vessels characteristic of Cappadocia at this period. The fine polychrome painted vessels of the 'Alishar III' type had come into their own with the foundation of the suburb at the turn of the second millennium and persisted throughout the first colony period (Level II). They were, however, afterwards, gradually replaced by the wonderfully graceful shapes of the later red or cream burnished wares ('Alishar II'), together with others, fantastically shaped, with excrescences in the form of birds and animals, which seem peculiar to Kültepe. For at this time the Anatolian craftsman's talent for modelling both in relief and in the round reached a high degree of ingenuity. There are religious subjects in which the iconography of the Plateau people alternates with that of neighbouring countries linked by trade; a lead figurine of a bearded Anatolian god with a conical headdress and a

Ill. 41

Ill. 45

Ills. 37, 44

Ills. 42, 43

Ills. 46, 47

Ills. 49, 50

49, 50 At Kültepe human figurines are depicted with less assurance than animals. *Left*, an ivory statuette; an Ishtar figure of the sort more closely associated with Syria than Mesopotamia; and (*right*) the head of a theriomorphic vase

sickle in his hand; a steatite mould for a relief, showing a family group of Anatolian deities, and in contrast to these a seated figure of a naked goddess with painted pubic triangle and hands supporting her breasts, which is more characteristically North Syrian. The conventionalized forms of animals are also popular and varied; single animals (a lion, an antelope or a reclining pig), serve as supports for clay goblets, or themselves serve as ritual pouring vessels. 'Rhyton' drinking cups are decorated with animals' heads, bulls, rams, pigs, dogs and rabbits all being represented.

The life of the *karum* at Kültepe is divided into two periods by some disaster which resulted in the destruction of the suburb by fire, after which it was rebuilt for the third time (Level Ib). Since we are now in the realm of written history, the approximate dates of these two occupations may be correlated with contemporary events in Assyria, by textual references to the names of kings and the eponymous magistracies of Ashur. In this way we find that the Level II occupation, which was the longer and more productive of the two, must have covered the reigns of Erishum, Sargon I and Puzur-Ashur (c. 1950–1850 BC), while Level Ib was contemporary with that of Shamsi-Adad I (c. 1825–1750 BC). But a new system is now

51 Impression of a cylinder-seal from a Kültepe tablet. The 'busy' and almost overcrowded design is characteristically Anatolian and among the motifs one recognizes the iconography of an indigenous religion. Anatolian deities, associated with their appropriate animals and ritual attributes, may be compared with those in the rock-reliefs at Yazilikaya (*Ill. 62*) dated five centuries later. This seal also bears a pictographic inscription

in use by which the Middle Bronze Age is divided into four sub-phases; the first covering the two pre-Assyrian occupations of the Kültepe suburb (Levels III and IV), the second corresponding to Level II and the third lasting until the destruction of the Level Ib *karum* in its turn by a fire which the colony did not survive. The fourth phase would then be taken to cover the interval between this event and the foundation of the Old Hittite Kingdom. The several occupations of the suburb find parallels in contemporary building-levels on the main mound, where the palaces of local rulers have occasionally produced vitally important cuneiform texts. The chronology of these too will presently be discussed.

One aspect of the finds in the *karum* is of importance, since it once more emphasizes the existence of an authentic Anatolian culture persisting through the vicissitudes of migration and political change. With the introduction of writing on clay tablets, the cylinder-seal also was adopted and the native inhabitants began to carve seals of their own. It is in the designs of these Anatolian seals that we first see the art and religious concepts of the indigenous people illustrated. For instance we see in them the iconography of the Anatolian gods, complete with their sacred furniture and ritual attributes, and we realize that these

Ill. 51

53

must have existed long before the advent of the Assyrians. Here already are the processions of deities mounted on their appropriate animals or on tiers of supporting figures of lesser rank. From now onwards these and other conventions will reappear as criteria of Anatolian tradition in the art of the Hittites and elsewhere. Primarily then we must infer that the Assyrians on their arrival in Anatolia did not enter a cultural void. They found themselves among a pattern of well-developed city communities with a pronounced character and long-established traditions of their own.

It is during the lifetime of the Assyrian colony at Kültepe that philologists have detected the presence in Central Anatolia of a people now conventionally known as the Hittites. The circumstances of their arrival and the process by which they adapted the traditions and resources of the country to their own requirements as an adolescent nation have long been a subject of study; but it is one which can hardly be discussed without some previous reference to the general linguistic situation in Anatolia at this time. This has until recently been much confused, not only by uncertainty regarding the identity of the varying dialects, but by a bewildering lack of agreement regarding the transliteration of the names applied to them. First then, to dispose of the pre-Indo-European languages, there is Akkadian ('Babylonian'), the international language of the time, and more locally there is the indigenous language of Central Anatolia, now known as Hattian ('Khattian', 'Hattic', 'Khattic'). Next, the Indo-European name used for the official language which we call 'Hittite' is a term literally meaning 'the language of the town of Nesha', the latter being identical with the name Kanesh (Kültepe). It might therefore, even more accurately, be called 'Kaneshite'. Finally, there are two other Indo-European dialects; Luvian ('Luwian') spoken as we have seen by immigrants into south-western

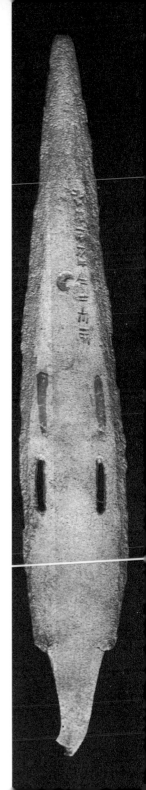

52 Discovered in an eighteenth-century setting on the main mound at Kültepe, a bronze spearhead bearing the inscription – 'Palace of Anitta, the King'; he was the first king to make Nesha (Kanesh), his capital

Anatolia late in the Early Bronze Age, written with the pictographs commonly called 'Hittite Hieroglyphs', and the more obscure 'Palaic', spoken probably in the northern district called Paphlagonia in classical times.

The first reliable testimony to the presence of Hittites at Kanesh during the period of the Assyrian colony was the occurrence of many recognizably Hittite names in the records kept by the merchants. For the rest, it was necessary to turn to the Hittites' own records of their earliest history, and particularly to the half-legendary 'Kings of Kussara' ('Kushshar'), from whom their heredity was supposed originally to be derived. An ancient document re-copied in the Hittite archives gave the name of a king called Pithana and of his son Anitta. No city called Kussara has yet been identified, but, included in an impressive list given by the text of cities which Pithana conquered was the name of Nesha (Kanesh) which his son, Anitta, had subsequently adopted as his capital. The authentic association of a king of this name with the early history of Kanesh has since been proved by the discovery in a public building on the mound at Kültepe of a bronze spearhead bearing the simple inscription, 'Palace of Anitta, the King', and more recently by the frequent readings of his name in texts, both from the Kanesh *karum* itself and from Alishar. From the archaeological context in which these texts were found we are also able to obtain some evidence suggesting an approximate date for the reign of Anitta. The excavator of Kültepe is satisfied that the 'Palace of Anitta' was destroyed by the same fire which brought to an end the second occupation (Level Ib) of the *karum*, an event which must be attributed to *c.* 1750 B C. Assuming that the Kings of Kussara were not themselves Hittites, there is now a tendency in some quarters to equate this or the previous destruction of the *karum* with a Hittite 'conquest'; but before accepting this interpretation, one should first consider whether this word is in fact compatible with the character of the political 'take-over' which the newcomers were in the process of contriving. Let us, therefore, consider their background.

One convincing argument for the arrival of the Hittites in Anatolia from a north-easterly direction is based on the burning or desertion during the twentieth century B C of a line of settlements representing the approaches to Cappadocia from that direction. This argument has been extended to account for a westward movement of peoples at that time, through the northern districts of the peninsula, ending with a change of population in the Troad and the Middle Helladic invasion of Greece. The evidence, however, from the Halys cities and Cappadocia does not conform to this picture of an invading army, destroying the settlements in its path and evicting their inhabitants. The impression gained is rather one of peaceful infiltration, leading by degrees to a monopoly of political power – like that of the Semitic Akkadians in the Sumerian world of Mesopotamia, or later of the Kassites in Babylonia. From their first appearance among the indigenous Anatolians, the two populations seem to have mingled freely, while the more flexible Neshian language gradually came to replace Hattian. Neither at this nor any later stage are the symptoms apparent of conscious nationalism or discrimination. What we do in fact watch is the assimilation by the Hittites of Anatolian traditions and practices. We see in their art and architecture, in their religion and iconography, many elements which are not of their own creation, but which emphasize their loyalty to principles adopted before their arrival. If we seek for qualities and predilections which may specifically be attributed to their own national heredity, we shall find them most obviously in their undoubted genius for military and political organization, in their talent for administration and their ambitious imperialism.

CHAPTER THREE

The Hittites

One of the few cities listed in the conquests of Anitta whose later identity can be recognized is Hattušaš, now known as Boghazköy. Its situation in the centre of the province enclosed by the curve of the Halys river must have been a strategic one, for an early Hittite king moved his capital thither from Kussara. Hattušaš from then onwards became the dynastic seat of the Hittite king-emperors and focal centre of their civilization. Excavations at Boghazköy resulted in the discovery of their official archives and from these the shape of Hittite history and civilization has since been reconstructed. The information emerging from the archives would today provide sufficient material for a history-book, complete with kings' names, numbered campaigns and dates of individual battles or treaties, as well as chapters on such subjects as social structure, economics, law and religion. This great volume of information is impossible to summarize usefully, and we shall therefore confine ourselves to assessing the cultural status of the Hittites among contemporary nations and their contribution to world civilization.

No historian would today be deceived by the magniloquent phraseology and extravagant claims with which the Hittite kings themselves adorned their records. Yet in the same records, minor episodes or incidental circumstances are occasionally mentioned with no apparent intention of impressing posterity, which nevertheless serve to convince one of the respect engendered by Hittite military prowess and political authority among the other powers of the contemporary scene. Even during the earlier phase of their history – the 'Old Kingdom' – there is the unquestionably authentic episode when Mursilis I, in a campaign whose success must have exceeded his wildest expectations, penetrated into Mesopotamia as far as the walls of Babylon and, finding its defences unprepared, entered the city and slew its Amorite king. Suddenly to find themselves masters in the Mesopotamian capital, amid the pomp and luxury associated with so great a centre of world civilization, must have astonished Mursilis and his simple highlanders almost to the point of embarrassment for they soon withdrew to a more familiar climate. Later, in the time of the 'Empire', there is also the attractive picture of Suppiluliumas, the greatest of Hittite conquerors, receiving the Egyptian envoys while encamped before Kadesh, and his almost incredulous bewilderment on understanding that they brought with them a request from their queen, the widow of Tut-ankh-amun, that one of his sons should become her husband. Such a marriage actually took place after the famous treaty made between the two kingdoms in 1269 BC, though in this case between a Hittite princess and an Egyptian Pharaoh.

Boghazköy

Perhaps the most effective testimony of all to the undoubted stature and ability of this Anatolian nation at the height of its political ascendancy and worldly aggrandizement is to be found in a different quarter altogether. A visit to the actual remains of the Hittite capital at Boghazköy, with its ruined palaces and temples,

53 A cuneiform tablet from the royal archives of the Hittites, found in the citadel (Büyükkale) of their capital at Hattušaš (Boghazköy). These tablets are written in the cuneiform script of Mesopotamia, but their language is that referred to by the Hittites themselves as 'Kaneshite', *i.e.* of the town of Kanesh (Kültepe). Yet it differs from the indigenous 'Hattian' of pre-Hittite Anatolia and also from other Indo-European dialects such as the Luvian of the 'Hittite' hieroglyphs

monumental sculptures and the four-mile circuit of its ponderously constructed walls cannot fail to leave one with the conviction that this city has been the cradle and home of a great imperial people.

The city spreads itself out on either side of a deep rocky gorge and looks northwards over a wide cultivated valley. The older part of the town is a mere four hundred yards long, mounting up to a high citadel. Here was the seat of government and in long store-rooms at some time destroyed by fire, the thousands of tablets composing the royal archive were brought to light. In 'Imperial' times the old city became inadequate and a vast extension was planned. Perhaps in the time of Suppiluliumas, a tremendous crescent of fortifications was flung up over the hillside to the south, making an enclosure which must have a total area of well over three hundred acres. Here the walls themselves present a prodigious feat of engineering for so early a period (fourteenth century BC). Their foundations are raised to a consistent level by a great rampart of earth, partly faced with a sloping wall of

Ill. 53

54 A relief sculpture from the door-jamb of the 'King's Gate' at Boghazköy, now in the Ankara Museum. It depicts a warrior wearing the Hittite 'kilt' and conical helmet with ear-flaps

dressed stone. Above this the sub-structure of the double wall which stands about thirty feet high is built of enormous stones, not laid in regular courses but meticulously joined. The brick structure above this has of course disappeared. There are chambered towers at short intervals, and in certain places outer 'apron' walls to prevent a direct attack. A postern or sally-port is created at one point by a stone vaulted tunnel passing beneath the rampart. There are five main gates with flanking towers, three of which have been named from the sculptures which adorn them – 'Sphinx', 'Lion' and 'King's Gate'.

Four buildings in the extended town have been identified as temples. One of them is an enormous limestone building with a colonnade facing on to a wide central court, and stands in a sacred enclosure or temenos enclosing an immense number of store-chambers and other subsidiary accommodation. In such buildings the actual sanctuary, which contained a cult-statue, is built of granite. It projects a little beyond the main façade in order to obtain lateral lighting for the statue.

Ill. 58

Ills. 55–57

The cult-figures themselves were missing from these temples, and elsewhere very few examples were found by the excavators of carving or modelling, so that our knowledge of Hittite art of this period is for the most part derived from two other sources, namely the portal sculptures adorning the city gates and from rock-reliefs in the neighbouring shrine at Yazilikaya. The most famous of the former is the 'warrior' from the King's Gate, now in the Ankara Museum. The figure is curiously impressive, though its importance consists more in the archaeological evidence which it presents of dress, weapons etc., than in actual artistic merit. The lion and sphinx figures too are primitive work and the interest of the latter lies mainly in the fact that the dual sculptures anticipate such features in Assyrian buildings by many centuries (and those at Persepolis by a thousand years).

Ills. 54–56

Ill. 54

The German excavations at Hattušaš are continued annually during the summer season, more recently concentrated mainly on the high acropolis of the old city, Büyükkale. Their object here has been the architectural analysis of the building remains; palaces, temples and storage-buildings with their arrangement of terraces and fortifications. Repeated rebuildings have retained the Anatolian tradition of binding together stone and mud brick in a framework of timber. Here too, the pottery and other objects seem hardly to have departed from precedents set by the inhabitants of Kanesh during the Assyrian colony period. In ceramics, there is still a preference for red polished surfaces with polychrome painted and inlaid details. A recent and rather dramatic find illustrating this technique was a pair of theriomorphic vases almost three feet high; bull-shaped libation vessels, whose form and purpose seems hardly to have changed in five hundred years. The only art-form which at the Hittite capital still seems conspicuously absent, though represented on a very small scale at Kültepe, is sculpture

55, 56 Portal-figure of a lion adorning a gateway to the outer city at Boghazköy. Here one sees the first appearance of an architectural convention, which culminated five centuries later in the 'lamassu' figures – winged bulls and lions guarding the entries to Assyrian palaces. Sphinxes, decorating another gate at Boghazköy are already designed as 'double-aspect' figures, their bodies extending into the reveal of the doorway

in the round. And this is perhaps due to a chance of survival since the much damaged remains of a colossal Hittite statue have now been found in an appropriate level at Alaca Hüyük.

Yazilikaya and Hittite Religion

By far the most interesting sculptures both from an artistic and a religious point of view, are the reliefs at Yazilikaya. This beautiful shrine is situated outside the city at a point where a spring of fresh water must once have discharged into a small valley shaded by trees. Deep clefts in the limestone, open to the sky and carpeted with grass and flowers, make a setting for the cult and the reliefs are carved on the vertical sides of two main recesses or 'chambers'. Outside them can be seen the ruins of an elaborately constructed entrance-gate, or propylon, through which they were approached. The outer chamber, which has traces of an altar-platform and was perhaps used for ceremonies such as the ratification of treaties, is decorated with a pageant of deities, some standing on

Ill. 61

Ills. 59, 60

57, 58 Walls and gateways of the
outer town at Boghazköy. The
gates themselves (*right*) and their
sculptures (*above*) form part of a
powerful substructure of stone,
above which the walls were built
in sun-dried brick. In the reconstruction *below* one sees the
outer 'apron-wall' which afforded
extra protection

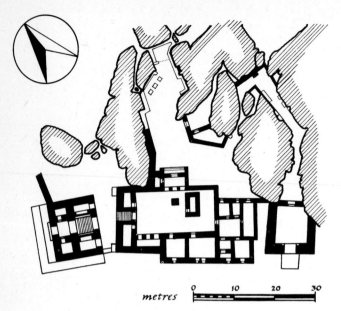

metres

0 10 20 30

Ill. 62

Ills. 64, 65

Ill. 67

their appropriate cult-animal or identified by a group of hieroglyphs. These figures are carved with no more than average proficiency; but those in the inner sanctuary are animated and infused with a religious emotion which craftsmanship alone could not have made articulate. The figure of a young king (identified as Tudhaliyas IV), in the protective embrace of a god is hardly less impressive than the symbolism of a huge dagger which appears thrust into the rock before him.

The Hittites were a practical, intellectually unpretentious people, devoid of the finer graces which adorned some other Near Eastern countries in their time. But they were born soldiers with great men to lead them and they were governed in peacetime by statesmen with a well-developed imperial policy. Also, religion seems to have played an important part in the conduct of their lives, and their beliefs were based on some curious concepts. One of the most remarkable scenes in the history of ceremonial ritual must have been enacted during their periodical festivals, when the priests and celebrants,

surrounded by helmeted guards and a throng of bullet-
headed townsmen, issued from the austerely monumental
public buildings of Hattušaš and converged on the cause-
ways leading up the adjoining valley to their mysterious
shrine. Life in their fortified mountain-gorge had made
them intuitively conscious of a mystery inherent in the
natural rocks which surrounded them; and it was perhaps among the clefts and caverns of Yazilikaya that their
sluggish emotions responded most easily to ritual
stimulation.

Ill. 60

Perhaps we have here for the first time contrived to lay
a finger on one metaphysical aspect of the Hittites which
served to distinguish them from their Hattic predecessors.
If so, we should go further and seek for any cultural or
political innovations, foreign to Anatolia, for which they
were responsible and which enabled them to lay the
imprint of Hittite nationality upon the history of the
period.

If we start then, for instance with the status of king-
ship, we shall find little to distinguish Hittite royalty from

65

61–63 The rock-cut sanctuary of the Hittites now known as Yazilikaya, a short distance outside the city-walls of Hattušaš. It is seen *above* from outside, and *below* are some of the relief sculptures of gods and goddesses with which it is ornamented. The central scene shows the Hurrian Weather-god, Teshub, standing upon images which represent deified mountains. Facing him is his consort Hepatu and her son Sarumma. Beneath, the procession of minor deities is prolonged around the side of the cave. They include figures from the Hurrian as well as the old Hattian pantheon and some are the patron gods of Hittite cities

64, 65 Two rock-reliefs from the inner chambers of the rock sanctuary at Yazilikaya. *Right, above*, on the east wall of chamber B, King Tudhaliyas IV is seen in the embrace of the young god. The king is simply dressed, wearing a round skull-cap and carrying the curved pastoral staff: above his head appears his own monogram in hieroglyphs beneath a winged sun-disc. The god wears a short tunic; his station is indicated by the tall conical horned headdress decorated with divided ellipses. On the east wall of chamber A this same king is once more depicted in relief (*below*). His mother, Puduhepa, wife of Hattusili III, was a Hurrian princess from Kizzuwatna, and during her lifetime the Hittite state cult was reorganized according to the Hurrian rite. This explains why the gods and goddesses depicted in the Yazilikaya sculptures all bear Hurrian names in hieroglyphic script

that of any other contemporary kingdom. It differed, at least from Egypt, in that the king was not in his lifetime deified, though this occasionally happened after his death. For the rest, his duty was to ensure the welfare of the state, to wage war and under certain circumstances to act as high priest. In the attendant political hierarchy, however, we are able to observe one feature which has aroused considerable interest simply because it does appear to be the expression of an exclusively Hittite political conception. This is the so-called *pankush* which, being literally interpreted as 'the whole community', has been taken to imply some sort of national assembly. But on closer examination, where privilege is concerned, one finds that a very large part of the ordinary population are excluded from this community. One is therefore immediately led to suspect the presence of an exclusive ruling caste; and, knowing the original role of the Hittites as Indo-European intruders among the indigenous Anatolians, to recognize in the *pankush* the mechanism of racial domination. Any criticism, by modern standards, of Hittite political practice which this may imply, is modified by the available evidence that this form of discrimination was short-lived. The fact that, during the final two hundred years of Hittite rule, no mention of the *pankush* appears in the texts, can hardly be a coincidence. Again a more sympathetic aspect of Hittite political idiosyncrasy is suggested by their liberal preference for diplomacy as an alternative to military action, and their humane treatment of their enemies in the event

66, 67 Two more relief sculptures from chamber B at Yazilikaya. On the east wall (*right*) are seen the relief of Tudhaliyas IV in the embrace of his god and near it, in the foreground, a figure which has come to be known as the 'Dirk God'; a colossal sword appears to be thrust into the rock, its hilt decorated with the figures of lions and terminating in the head of a god wearing a horned headdress. The symbolism of this device is unexplained but its appearance most impressive. Opposite this, on the west wall (*left*), is a procession of twelve identical gods moving in single file

of military victory. As an example of the former, one might cite their predilection for arranging royal marriages, while the latter is confirmed by the total absence in their records of any reference to punitive brutality or deterrent 'frightfulness' such as that in which the Assyrians later specialized. The superior social status of women was another feature of the Hittite régime which appears to suggest liberality of outlook.

In the end, however, one comes to the conclusion that it is in the art of the Hittites, less in its subject matter than its style and in the conventions which dictate its imagery, that one recognizes the criteria and hallmark of their collective individuality. The rigid and distinctive conventions of Hittite imagery seem to have crystallized into a canonical formula during the early decades of the Empire in the late fifteenth century and to have been retained almost without variation till the régime ended.

68 Guarding the gateway to the Hittite city at Alaca Hüyük, portal figures in the form of sphinxes, carved partly in the round. Judging from the relief sculptures with which the adjoining walls are adorned, this whole group must represent some of the earliest examples of architectural sculpture in imperial Hittite times

The iconography and allusive symbolism of old Anatolian religious beliefs and rituals may, as we have said, have been scrupulously preserved and they may have been supplemented by accretions from alien sources such as the Hurrians with whom the Hittites were now perpetually in contact; but their representation, whether modelled in clay, cast in metal or sculptured in stone, now conformed to a code of prescribed imagery which stamped it as authentically Hittite.

The inventory of surviving antiquities and monuments on which this argument is based is not, in fact, very voluminous and some of the most outstanding examples have already been enumerated. First and foremost of course, at Hattušaš itself, are the reliefs in the rock shrine of Yazilikaya and the portal sculptures at the gates of the extended city which date from the Empire period. But there are other examples and categories of Hittite art which have not yet been mentioned. There is a surviving gateway in the wall of the Empire-period city at Alaca

69 Unconventional subjects are represented among the wall reliefs at Alaca Hüyük; wild animals, hunted or in conflict, drawn with a freedom and in a style not normally associated with Hittite art

Hüyük where the Early Bronze Age tombs were found; and here, in association with the much-weathered portal figures in the form of sphinxes and lions, are orthostats, which are carved in relief, sometimes with secular subjects. This must be one of the earliest examples yet known of this architectural device, since for the most part they are sculptured on the actual blocks of masonry rather than on upright slabs as the name 'orthostat' implies. In any case they constitute a distinctive group both in style and subject-matter. Apart from the more conventional scenes of religious worship, they include figures of animals – lion, stag, bull and boar – hunted or in conflict, as well as a group of performing jugglers. They are carved, on basalt in very flat relief, the figures only slightly modelled and depending on the fine calligraphic outlines of the stylized animal forms.

In a rather different category are the rock-reliefs and other monuments of the period, scattered fairly widely over central and south-western Anatolia. Some of them,

Ill. 68

Ill. 69

71

which fall within the 'home-counties' of the Hittite kingdom, are undoubtedly the work of the Hittites themselves
and in certain cases are associated by hieroglyphic inscriptions with the names of actual kings. This group
includes the relief of King Muwattali on its rock overlooking the river at Sirkeli, near Adana in the Hittite
province of Kizzuvatna; the two great rock-cut figures at
Ill. 70 Gavurkalesi, near Ankara, where there is also a masonry-
built Hittite tomb; and a much-weathered religious scene
on a rock at Fraktin, near Kayseri. There are others
which, rather disconcertingly, fall outside the geographical area over which the Hittite kings had any, or
at all permanent political control. They include the royal
reliefs at Karabel, near Izmir, and the 'Mother of the
Gods' on Mount Sipylos, near Manisa, as well as the
Ill. 73 masonry-built shrine at Eflatun Pinar, beside Lake
Beyşehir and the stone statue found near by at Fasillar,
about which we shall have more to say. The Karabel
relief indeed has an inscription in 'Hittite' hieroglyphs,
but these do not give the names of known Hittite kings,
and, as has been mentioned elsewhere, these hieroglyphs
were in fact a vehicle for the Luvian dialect – the language
spoken in the kingdom of Assuwa, within whose territory the monument lies. Where, therefore, scholars have
in the past tended to explain these sculptures as victory
monuments commemorating Hittite conquests, their
general proximity to some form of water-supply has more
recently led them to be associated with a 'spring-cult' or
some other religious institution. Furthermore, since a
distinction can be drawn between this very ancient Anatolian concept of 'water-from-the-earth', on the one hand,
and on the other, that of 'water-from-the-sky', associated
with the Indo-European mountain- and weather-gods,
this might again suggest pre-Hittite inspiration for the
Assuwan monuments. In this case, however, it has to
be admitted that, in the details of these sculptures, the

70 Rock relief carved beneath a Hittite fortress at Gavurkalesi between Ankara and Hymana in central Anatolia. Two gods appear whose horned headdresses show them to be of different rank

unmistakable criteria of Hittite imagery would be difficult to explain.

Considering the extent and prolongation of excavations at the site of the Hittite capital and elsewhere, the representation of small-scale figurative art in materials such as metal, stone or ivory is deplorably, and indeed inexplicably scanty. Here we can do hardly more than mention a male statuette in bronze from Boghazköy and a tiny gold figure of the same sort in the British Museum. There remains the category of engraved seals, few of which have been actually found but many of which are known from their impressions on clay. In this case, cylinder-seals of the Mesopotamian type are extremely rare. The Hittites used stamp-seals, usually conical affairs with a flat base surmounted by a ring or perforated boss for purposes of suspension. The seal itself could be cylindrical or even square, in which case subsidiary designs could also be

Ill. 72

Ill. 71

71 Seal-impression of a Hittite gold ring, showing a god standing upon an appropriate animal between two lions

72 Miniature figure in gold of a Hittite king, now in the British Museum

carved on the sides. The main design consisted of a central field containing a pattern of hieroglyphs and symbols from a repertoire identical with that to be found in the sculptured reliefs, and this was surrounded by a border of guilloche or other ornament and sometimes a cuneiform inscription. Royal seals incorporated the king's 'monogram' again as in the reliefs.

We should now perhaps consider in detail the conventions – both graphic and formal – which as we have said constitute the recognizable criteria of Hittite imagery, in all these monuments. And it should be said at once that these can be conveniently and reliably identified from whatever geographical provenance a Hittite work of art may be derived. To illustrate this, one need only cite the case of a bronze statuette from Latakiya in the Louvre or the beautiful gold *cloisonné* inlays from a fourteenth-century tomb at Carchemish. By contrast one might point to a male figurine from Tokat in the Hittite homeland, to which, dating as it does from the sixteenth century B C, the imperial conventions have not yet been applied.

Ill. 76
Ill. 77

Ill. 75

73, 74 The masonry-built shrine erected over a spring at Eflatun Pinar near Beyşehir (*above*), as it appears today, bearing much weathered reliefs, probably representing the Hittite pantheon. Recently associated with this monument is a giant statue of a god, removed from its original setting and found at Fassilar, thirty miles away (see reconstruction *right*)

75, 76 Rare examples of Hittite figurative art in metal. *Left*, a bronze figurine of a god from Tokat, dating from the sixteenth century BC and not yet fully adapted to Hittite conventions. *Right*, a similar statuette from Latakiya, now in the Louvre, which conforms more closely to the precepts of Hittite art

77 Component pieces from some large art-work, found in a fourteenth-century tomb at Carchemish. This form of inlay, called '*cloisonné*', consists of small compartments separated by ribbons of gold and filled with vitreous enamel. Two of the figures are kings, carrying the curved pastoral staff

For an examination, then, of the conventions themselves, the Yazilikaya reliefs might prove a convenient point of departure. Here we see, though in minority representation, the appearance of ordinary mortals; the male with a beard but no moustache, a single ear-ring and hair either short or in a pigtail. Mortal or god, the male wears a belted tunic ending above the knee and sometimes a longer cloak over it. Whatever weapons or insignia are carried he holds one arm extended in front of him and the other bent at the elbow against his chest. Anatolian boots with upturned toes are also the rule. Women hold both arms extended, but one is bent upwards in a beckoning gesture. Both gods and goddesses of superior grade stand upon appropriate animals or on supporting minor deities. This is an age-old formula in Anatolia which we have seen in the cylinder-seals of Kültepe and which in fact has its roots in the Chalcolithic or Neolithic concepts of Hacılar and Çatal Hüyük. More significant are, for instance, their headdresses, which are distinctively Hittite. Gods wear the conical fluted cap ornamented with horns, which vary in number and position according to their status. That of the supreme god only is also decorated with the divided ellipses which are divine ideograms. All carry weapons or implements

Ill. 62

Ill. 62

Ill. 66
Ills. 72, 75

which are their special attributes. Goddesses normally wear a cylindrical 'polos' or a flattened conical cap; but those at Yazilikaya have a 'mural crown' which is also worn by the Earth Mother of the Sipylos monument. They too wear belted tunic and skirt, pleated robes of this sort being characteristic. By contrast to the gods, kings wear a simple round skull-cap, horns being a symbol only of posthumous deification, and carry the curved pastoral staff, now identified with the Hittite word *kalmush*. Their figures are usually distinguished by one or more winged sun-discs, beneath which their 'monograms' appear in hieroglyphs.

Ill. 65

The chief divinity of the Hittites, the Weather-God, was held in equal respect by the Indo-European and the autochthonous sections of the population. He was perhaps to be identified with Adad, the Mesopotamian god of thunder, by whose ideogram his name is usually represented in the texts. The Hurrians called him Teshub. His proper attribute is the bull, mounted upon which he appears in so many Hittite sculptures, and indeed reappears in Roman mythology under the name of Jupiter Dolichenus. As for the great mother-goddess of Anatolian antiquity whom the Greeks know as Cybele, she was adopted by the Hittites from the old Hattic pantheon, but her antecedents have now been traced by archaeology in the Stone Age. The Hittites worshipped her as the Sun Goddess of Arinna, but in the mixed iconography of Yazilikaya she seems to be merged with the Hurrian goddess Hepat into a single composite deity. There were minor gods and goddesses, many of whom can be recognized at Yazilikaya, including the group of twelve, twice represented there, whose names are not recorded in the texts.

It is perhaps the two central figures of the Hittite pantheon who are represented in the sculptured relief at Eflatun Pinar to which we have already referred. If so,

Ill. 73

an interesting corollary is to be inferred from a recent attempt to reconstruct its appearance. Here undoubtedly we are dealing with a spring-cult, for the masonry-built altar (or platform as it should perhaps be called), faces the source of a stream running into Beyşehir Lake. Just recognizable on the face of the stone, beneath winged sun-discs are figures including a god and seated goddess: but there are also scattered fragments of some sort of upper structure, including apparently one which can be identified as part of a stone lion or leopard. These fragments have recently been reconsidered in conjunction with the remains of another monument also of trachyte stone, the giant statue lying on a hillside at Fassilar, thirty miles away. The Fassilar statue, almost unique as an example of Hittite sculpture in the round, lies among the ruins of a small classical city to which it seems likely to have been carried as a trophy. Roughly sculptured and thought by some to be unfinished, it takes the shape of a god with appropriate head-dress and one arm upraised, and it is supported by the engaged figures of two lions also carved partly in the round. One scholar has now suggested that this statue and the pedestal at Eflatun might in fact be parts of the same monument. By the process of mounting the one on top of the other (a process which might almost be compared to superimposing the Albert Memorial on the Albert Hall), he has contrived the most impressive not to say convincing reconstruction, in which the god and seated goddess of the relief are repeated by more monumental figures above, each with its supporting beasts.

Ill. 74

Having mentioned Assuwa, let us now take a further look at the other neighbouring states. A good deal is known from the Boghazköy records about neighbouring states, against which the Hittite kings waged war, or with whom they had more peaceful connections; and on the map their location, inferred from the textual evidence, is shown in such a way as to be comparable with the rather less equivocal division of the country into cultural provinces delimited by archaeological research. Some controversy still persists in regard to the placing of Ahhiyawa, because this name was applied by the Hittites to a people who in the past have often been identified with the Achaeans of Homeric legend. But archaeologists, finding that the Ahhiyawa homeland can be located on the Anatolian mainland without violating any logical inference from the texts, have recently begun to favour a new theory regarding this north-western province. It may, they consider, have been from here that the first true Greeks crossed the Aegean to colonize the European mainland at the beginning of the second millennium BC. According to this theory, the Ahhiyawans were themselves recent arrivals, having appeared from the west simultaneously with the arrival of the Hittites from the east. By this process of reasoning the Ahhiyawans would have been a proto-Greek people who remained on the Anatolian mainland during the centuries in which their own colonists were creating the Mycenaean commune in the Aegean. This would explain the close ties between the Mycenaean merchants and the Trojans of the sixth settlement – a facility not enjoyed by the Assuwans of the central Aegean coast who were an Anatolian people and perhaps distrustful of the Greeks.

At this point we should perhaps remind ourselves that, by the time the Achaean Greeks organized the expedition against the city of Troy described by Homer, the events mentioned in the Hittite records were already becoming historical. The best known date, computed by the Greek chronologists of later times, for the fall of Troy (and one which archaeologists find most easy to accept), is 1192 BC. By that time, if any reliance is to be placed on Homer's list of Priam's allies, the political scene in the Troad and its hinterland was in the process of fairly rapid change.

The area we have tentatively identified as the Late Bronze Age state of Ahhiyawa could hardly have remained unaffected by the eastward migrations across the straits, which were now beginning to take place at regular intervals. Nevertheless, the survival of an Ahhiyawan element in the population of Priam's Troy would explain the cultural affinity which Homer envisages between the Trojans and the Greeks. It is a pity that no light was thrown on this subject by the excavations of the Homeric settlement at Troy itself (settlement VII A), whose remains had been largely destroyed by later foundations.

Turning to Arzawa, a state with which the Hittite kings seem to have been continually at war without effecting any permanent conquest, there is evidence from the excavations at Beycesultan to show that the city there partially excavated may, during the Middle Bronze Age, have had the dignity of a state-capital. Amongst other buildings dating from this period (1900–1750 BC), a remarkably large palace was brought to light, planned in a way which partly resembled those of Minoan Crete and elaborately constructed of brick and timber on a stone foundation. Its unusual amenities included a system of sub-pavement passages, presumably for circulating hot air in the winter; and though the destruction of the building by fire after looting, perhaps during one of the early Hittite wars, has destroyed much other valuable evidence, one gains the impression that the Arzawans were a people of wealth and dignity. There was also a walled enclosure full of large administrative buildings of a sort which would have justified the expectation of written archives. The fact that no inscribed material was found, though there is reason to believe that Arzawa at this time fell within the area inhabited by an Indo-European people, speaking and writing the Luvian dialect, has led to some speculation regarding the use of writing materials other than clay tablets, which might have perished.

Ill. 78

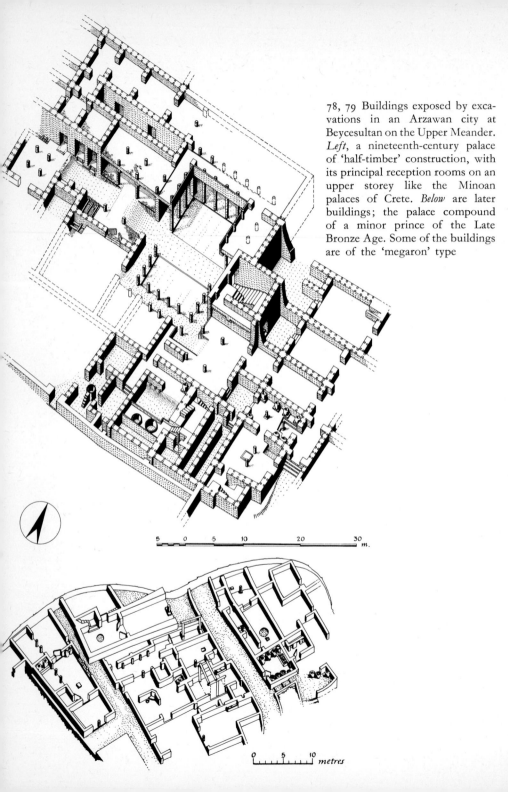

78, 79 Buildings exposed by excavations in an Arzawan city at Beycesultan on the Upper Meander. *Left*, a nineteenth-century palace of 'half-timber' construction, with its principal reception rooms on an upper storey like the Minoan palaces of Crete. *Below* are later buildings; the palace compound of a minor prince of the Late Bronze Age. Some of the buildings are of the 'megaron' type

5 0 5 10 20 30 m.

0 5 10 metres

80 In a Late Bronze Age shrine at Beycesultan, a 'horned altar' of terracotta with a ritual hearth beside it and votive vessels in the foreground. As in the Early Bronze Age levels at this site, here also the shrines are arranged in pairs, perhaps having a dual dedication to male and female deities

In the Late Bronze Age, the city at Beycesultan lost its importance and became the seat of a small feudal prince. His palace compound which was partly excavated contained residences in the form of 'megara' and elaborate stabling accommodation for horses. Elsewhere a religious shrine with a 'horned altar' once more recalled Minoan symbolism.

Ill. 79

Other states appearing on the map, apart from the so-called Upper and Lower Lands which fall both historically and archaeologically within the sphere of direct Hittite influence, include Kizzuvatna, over which the Hittite kings usually maintained a fairly tight control since it covered the lines of communication for campaigns in Syria. At the end of the Early Bronze Age a people called Hurri, coming from the neighbourhood of Lake Urmia, had established themselves as a ruling class in this area, and it was the Hurrian wife of King Tudhaliyas IV who had been responsible for introducing an alien element into the pantheon depicted in the reliefs at Yazilikaya. An offshoot from Hurrian stock had also at this time created the important state of Mitanni, whose territory extended into northern Assyria. Apart from these, the most active though historically obscure people were the barbaric Kaskaeans of Pontus and Paphlagonia, who seemed perpetually to be creating a 'second front' in the Hittite wars.

CHAPTER FOUR

The Neo-Hittite States

The Hittite Empire came to an end almost simultaneously with the fall of Troy and the beginning of the Iron Age. In the opening years of the first millennium B C, Phrygians from Thrace swept the country as far as the north-western slopes of Taurus and destroyed the imperial strongholds on the Halys.

The political history of the Hittite nation did not end with the destruction of Hattušaš and the expulsion of its people from their homeland in Anatolia. Driven southward from the cities and pasturelands of the plateau, they descended through Anti-Taurus into the valley of the upper Euphrates and pressed on further into the plains of north Syria. These were familiar lands to them; for their rulers had long been vassals of the Hittite kings and the cities had paid tribute to the imperial treasury. Several national elements now composed their population: Aramaeans from the tribal lands in the south, families of Hurrians and expatriate Hittites, once concerned with imperial administration and trade. These latter now gained political ascendancy and the cities, particularly the old provincial capitals such as Carchemish and Sinjerli, soon resumed the semblance of Hittite principalities, though the non-Hittite element in their internal composition preserved for each its individual and independent character. So the imperial régime was succeeded in the Early Iron Age by a strange historical aftermath, during which the Hittite world became no more than a constellation of small and disunited city-states, striving by miscellaneous alliances to maintain their independence on the periphery of the Assyrian Empire.

Curiously enough this period of five centuries, during which the cities in fact often became vassals of the Assyrians or were subjected to non-Hittite rule when the Aramaean element in their population got the upper hand, has bequeathed to us a far greater heritage of archaeological remains than the imperial régime which preceded it. The whole accumulation from this source creates a curious picture of a hybrid civilization, spreading over a wide geographical area, which does not conform to any conventionally defined province in later times. The linguistic diversity of the inscriptions and the complex evidence of foreign influence on sculptural style, provide a clue to the political insecurity and unstable fortunes of the states themselves.

Hittite Picture-Writing

The period is sometimes known as 'Neo-Hittite' or 'Syro-Hittite'; and the cities not already mentioned include Marash, Sakçagözü and, on the fringe of the plateau, Malatya. Some of them have been partially excavated and their public buildings have yielded, in addition to statues, large quantities of stone slabs, sculptured in relief in a style showing much foreign influence. The content of the pictures and that of rock reliefs dating from this period, like the one at Ivriz, is often supplemented by inscriptions in a form of pictographic writing which the Hittites had inherited from an earlier stage in their cultural history. It was in fact the original vehicle for one of the Indo-European dialects from which the Hittite language was composed, but when these excavations took

81, 82 At Ivriz, on the northern side of the Taurus range, a rock-relief is carved where a river gushes out of the hillside to irrigate a fertile oasis of fruit and vegetable gardens. Here depicted is a local ruler of the late eighth century BC, a contemporary of Tiglath-pileser III, paying homage to a god of fertility. The style of the carving shows Hittite, Assyrian and Aramaean influence

83 Ruined gateway of a Neo-Hittite prince's country palace overlooking the Ceyhan valley and the plain of Cilicia at Karatepe

place it had not been deciphered. But inscriptions in Aramaic and Phoenician do also occasionally occur alongside the hieroglyphs, and it was the discovery of a bi-lingual text of this sort in 1947 which eventually made the decipherment of the pictographs possible. The discovery was made at a place called Karatepe on the banks of the Ceyhan river, where it breaks down through a rocky valley into the plain of Cilicia. An eighth-century *Ill. 83* princeling, describing himself as a vassal of the king of Adana, had here built himself a fortified country palace with formally designed gateways which, in the fashion of the time, he ornamented with sculptured reliefs. The *Ills. 85, 86* sculptures (whose preservation *in situ* the Turkish government has contrived) show a conspicuously low standard of workmanship and a most perplexing confusion of styles; but there is a long and informative inscription repeated on either side of the main entrances, first in

84 An example of 'Hittite hieroglyphic' writing, whose understanding has been much facilitated by the discovery at Karatepe of a bi-lingual inscription with the hieroglyphic text repeated in Phoenician. These pictographs were originally the vehicle for an Indo-European dialect known as 'Luvian'

Ill. 84

Hittite hieroglyphs, and then in Phoenician. Since the Phoenician script is already well understood, the 'crib' which is thus conveniently provided to the hieroglyphs has been welcomed, like the Rosetta Stone or the Behistun inscriptions in an earlier generation, as a linguistic key which may give access to a whole new literature. But one must hasten to add that this hope has not yet altogether been fulfilled. It often takes a very long time for philologists to decipher a script, even after all the necessary evidence has been collected. Meanwhile, our knowledge of Syro-Hittite history continues to depend for the most part on the dim reflection of events and personalities which is to be found in the Assyrian annals.

Art and Architecture

Let us now give some attention to the diverse and complicated subject of stylistic developments and influences in the art of the Hittite 'diaspora'. In doing so we shall find our view of the material available limited almost

85, 86 Relief sculptures from the palace gates at Karatepe. Here again the Assyro-Aramaean influence is more prominent than the Hittite, and even Egyptian motifs are occasionally recognizable. The orthostat slabs are often badly matched both in size and style. In the banqueting scene (*above*), the musicians on the left have hair and beards dressed in the Assyrian manner, while the servants attending a feast on the right wear typically Aramaean caps. These reliefs represent a crude and rather hybrid form of art and were probably executed by craftsmen of several different nationalities

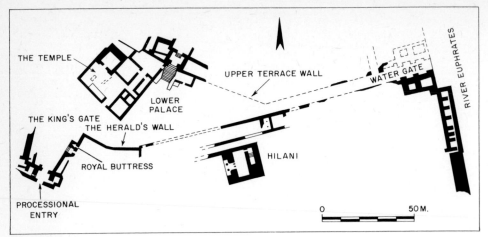

87, 88 Plan (*above*) of the principal public buildings of the Neo-Hittite period, excavated at Carchemish on the Euphrates. A processional entry on the south-west side leads to an irregular-shaped piazza, and beyond a wide stairway leads up to the high citadel above (not excavated). From the piazza, a street also leads down eastward to a gateway in the quay-wall, perhaps the oldest building of all. The wealth of the sculptures recovered from Carchemish are mainly orthostats which decorated the walls of the piazza inside the processional entry. *Right*, the appearance of a river-side fortress such as Carchemish is suggested by a scene depicted on one of the famous bronze gates of Shalmaneser III discovered at Balawat near Nimrud

exclusively to sculpture in stone: nor will our study be much concerned with its aesthetic appraisal, since neither the details of its design nor its overall efficacy as an architectural ornament can be said to invite comparison with the higher forms of contemporary art in the Near East. This being so, we shall also have again to remind ourselves that, up to the second decade of the present century, it was by this material alone that the cultural status of the Hittite nation could be judged. First, then, to consider the excavated cities and other sources from which Neo-Hittite antiquities are derived, one should start with the two which have been most thoroughly explored, namely Carchemish and Sinjerli.

Ill. 88

The site of Carchemish is fitted neatly into a bend of the Euphrates at a point which at present coincides with the Turco-Syrian frontier. The fortified city of Hittite times is an oval extension in a south-westerly direction of the citadel on its ancient mound, and there is a further extension in the form of a walled outer city. Any Hittite

buildings which existed on the citadel itself have been made inaccessible by later occupations; so the British excavations were mainly concerned with those surrounding an open piazza at the approach to the old mound on the south side. The entrance to the piazza from the city in the south was through the 'King's Gate', inside which, on the right-hand wall, was a group of sculptures which included something called the 'Royal Buttress'. At right-angles to this and running eastwards was another range of slabs known as the 'Herald's Wall', after which one turned left to face a gateway and stair leading to the mound and saw on one's left a third group called the 'Long Wall of Sculptures'. Finally a long enclosed street led down eastwards to the Water Gate on the river quay and here were some of the oldest sculptures of all, carved on structural blocks of masonry. All the Carchemish sculptures are derived from these various groups.

Other buildings adjoining the piazza were, to the west a simply planned temple and to the south a reception-suite,

Ill. 87

Ill. 90

Ill. 91

conforming to the plan of what has come to be called a *bît hilani*. The 'hilani' is an architectural convention which is now conclusively proved to be of Syrian origin. Its only association with the Hittites is due to a confusion of terms in an inscription of King Sargon II, who attributed its invention to the 'Hatti' (of the diaspora). Nevertheless, since we shall encounter it again at Sinjerli and elsewhere, it should perhaps be described. It consists in fact of a single, integral group of chambers, of which the indispensable elements are – a single axial entrance through a columned portico into a rectangular reception-hall, a staircase leading to the roof, usually at one end of the hall, and certain retiring-rooms behind. The portico columns were of wood and required the support of a substantial stone base. This provided the *raison d'être* for a characteristic feature of Neo-Hittite architectural sculpture, which often took the form of paired beasts; lions or bulls.

90, 91 Above, relief sculptures decorating the so-called 'Royal Buttress' (*see* plan, *Ill. 87*) facing the 'King's Gate' at Carchemish. In a panel on the left one sees King Araras, a ruler of Carchemish late in the eighth century B C, and his son Kamanas. Carrying a child and leading an animal of some species is the King's wife, Luwarisas, right, and between the two are other members of the same family. *Below* is the so-called 'Long Wall of Sculptures' with reliefs representing the Syrian 'naked goddess', the god Teshub, warriors riding in chariots, armed infantry and some slabs entirely covered by inscriptions

Regarding the sculptured orthostats themselves, it has already been said that they are artistically unimpressive. In the first place the slabs are small – seldom more than three feet high – while the sculpture is technically immature and the designs ill-balanced. Where the reliefs of Imperial times were carved on white limestone or trachyte of a fairly superior quality, the fashion became prevalent in Neo-Hittite times of alternating such limestone slabs with others of the black basalt which is so plentifully available in North Syria. This latter is a hard stone of irregular composition and the Hittite sculptors were compelled to adapt their technique to its unresponsive character; one suspects that in this way their standards of refinement in carving were gradually lowered. As for the subjects of the designs there seems to have been a free choice between religious and secular scenes, with a slight preference for the latter. At Carchemish, one might

Ill. 91

take the Long Wall as typical; a procession of gods, chariots and warriors, carved on a motley array of black and white slabs which extend for a distance of over a hundred feet. One of the first figures one recognizes is Teshub, the Hurrian weather-god, next to whom, seen in full face, is an unclothed female figure with hands supporting her breasts, which one recognizes as the Syrian

Ill. 92

'Naked Goddess', last mentioned here when discussing the Kültepe cylinder-seals of a thousand years earlier. In this case she has wings and her body is enclosed in the outline of a veil. After her come a number of slabs repre-

Ill. 89

senting warriors riding in chariots, a slab covered with a hieroglyph inscription and a line of infantry bringing in prisoners.

The 'Herald's Wall' is really a round-the-corner continuation of the sculptures in the 'King's Gate' and belongs to the same series. But here it is more difficult to detect any coherent plan behind the arrangement of subjects. Their understanding is further hampered both by

92, 93 More reliefs from the walls of the piazza at Carchemish. *Above*, details of the 'Long Wall of Sculptures' including the Syrian 'naked goddess' with wings and the outline of a veil. *Below*, a group of musicians with horn and large drum. The coarse texture of the black basalt is well seen in these pictures

94 Statue in the round of a seated god with beard and horned headdress. It is mounted on a wide base composed of two lions, also partly carved in the round. The statue itself was destroyed during the First World War, but the base survives in the Ankara Museum, minus the head of one lion which is in the British Museum. In Neo-Hittite architecture, bases like this one with paired beasts are often used to support stout wooden columns (cf. *Ill. 98*)

their poor state of preservation and by the fact that they have clearly been replaced and rearranged during improvements to the piazza carried out by a succession of kings. They include a banqueting scene, a group of musicians and a procession of acolytes among whom are priestesses wearing a veil or cloak draped over their high 'polos' headgear. They bring offerings to Kubaba, the protective deity of Carchemish, who is similarly dressed but sits with her back to the procession. At Carchemish, it remains only to mention one well-known example of contemporary sculpture in the round; the statue of a huge seated god with square beard and horned headdress. He is supported on a pair of lions and the space between them, in the Mesopotamian manner, is filled by a relief-carving of a beaked hybrid. In a similar group

Ill. 93

Ill. 95

Ill. 96

Ill. 94

95, 96 Sculptures from the so-called 'Herald's Wall' in the piazza at Carchemish. On the right, part of a procession of priestesses wearing veils draped over the cylindrical 'polos' headdress. They bring offerings to Kubaba, the protective deity of Carchemish, recognizable by the pomegranate which is her symbol. The careless arrangement of these sculptures is emphasized by the fact that she has her back to the procession

found at Sinjerli, the tall figure of a king stands upright on a lion-base, with which he appears uncomfortably out-of-scale.

Ill. 98

At Sinjerli, the German excavations revealed public buildings grouped inside a fortified citadel with inner and outer gateways, once more raised upon the summit of an ancient mound. In this case the citadel is entirely surrounded by an extensive outer city, enclosed in a double line of towered walls which form a perfect circle. In the citadel there is an 'Upper' and a 'Lower Palace' creating a complex of buildings which include at least four separate 'hilani' units. But at this site the sculptures seem mainly to have been used as decoration for the gates and gate-chambers. Their style will presently be discussed in connection with the increasing evidence here apparent of

Ill. 100

97–99 Sculptures from Sinjerli (ancient Sam'al), including (*left*) a stela of the Assyrian king Esarhaddon (681–669 BC), and (*right*) a standing figure of a god on a pedestal of paired lions. Below, the Aramaean ruler, Barrekub, speaks with his scribe, seated upon a typical Assyrian throne (*cf. Ill. 111*)

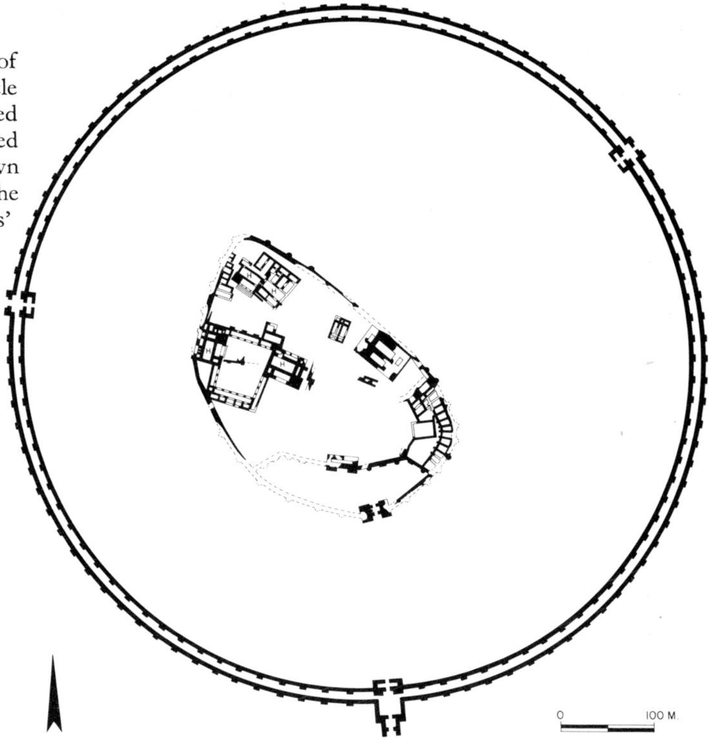

100 Plan of the city of Sinjerli with a double circle of outer city-walls, walled citadel with doubly fortified entry and buildings, known to the excavators as the 'Upper and Lower Palaces'

0 ___ 100 M.

Assyrian influence. Among their subjects, characteristic features not previously observed at Carchemish are the actual portraits of royalty, sometimes identified by inscriptions and occupying a single slab or stela in some conspicuous position. The most famous of these is the figure of Barrekup, an Aramaean ruler of the city, whom we see seated on a very characteristically Assyrian throne, in conversation with his principal scribe.

Ill. 97

Ill. 99

The contrasting geographical situations of Sinjerli and Carchemish – the one in a typical Anatolian alpine valley and the other on the fringes of the Mesopotamian plain – is interestingly reflected in the structural principles of building in the two cities. We have already mentioned elsewhere the Anatolian practice of reinforcing stone and mudbrick houses with a substantial framework of timber, though not perhaps the belief, now well established, that this device was introduced as a precaution against earthquakes. In any case, we do find at Sinjerli walls which incorporate so high a proportion of timber that the brick and stone have become mere incidental filling, whereas at Carchemish, on a solid stone substructure corresponding to the height of the orthostats, the walls consist of unreinforced brick-work. The fact that Carchemish is situated just beyond the limits of a geographical zone subject to earthquakes need not be a coincidence. Other sites within the danger zone from which Neo-Hittite sculpture is derived – Sakçagözü, for instance, the small palace establishment near Sinjerli, and Tell Taynat, near Antioch – both show half-timber construction, while isolated orthostats discovered at Marash and elsewhere may be from buildings destroyed in such natural disasters.

Ill. 101

In referring to the 'Hittite' hieroglyphs which often supplement the relief carving on Neo-Hittite orthostats, we have mentioned how, in particular at Carchemish, their decipherment has made it possible to reconstruct a reasonably coherent genealogy of local rulers of whose reigns the approximate dates can be estimated. The co-ordination with these dates of uninscribed sculptures, according to a chronology of stylistic developments, has proved a far more difficult task – a task which must incidentally have been rendered doubly difficult for the excavators themselves by the lack of comparative material. It has, however, more recently been attempted by a Turkish scholar, with a high proportion of the actual works themselves at hand for closer study. Professor E. Akurgal's conclusions on the subject are satisfyingly well-substantiated and, with only minor reservations, are at present generally accepted. Briefly, he makes an overall division of the designs into categories, according to the preponderant stylistic influences by which they are characterized, and he demonstrates how these can be adapted to a chronological pattern. Taking as a point of departure a 'traditional' style still dependent on memories of Imperial times, he distinguishes two successive phases

101 Relief slab from Carchemish carved with typical Hittite hieroglyphs. It was the discovery of bi-lingual inscriptions at Karatepe (*Ill. 84*) that facilitated the understanding of this writing

of increasing Assyrian influence, each corresponding to a period of territorial expansion in the history of the Mesopotamian state, and in the second phase, notes the simultaneous accretion of unorthodox ideas from Aramaean and other North Syrian sources. And here at once we begin to understand the complexity of the analyst's task. For we cannot forget that 'traditional' Hittite art, beneath its uniform veneer of Imperial imagery, is itself a composite affair, in which Hurrian-Mitannian elements from North Syria are already superimposed on a basically Anatolian substructure. Nevertheless, Akurgal's 'traditional' style of later times does emerge as a valid determination.

The association of an actual chronology with this conservative style has presented a new difficulty. Scholars have found it impossible to agree on an upper date-limit for the revival of Hittite art in the 'diaspora'. One would expect this to coincide with the years following the exodus from the imperial 'homeland' in the twelfth century BC: but it has, on the contrary, been fashionable until quite recently to postulate a 'Dark Age' of several centuries following this event, dating from which no cultural remains (either Hittite or Phrygian) are outstanding. Where Syria is concerned, this theory has been rejected by excavators, who find evidence of continuity in the archaeological remains of the period. But nothing of this sort has been found in the Anatolian area. To illustrate this we may consider one of the most authentically 'traditional' and therefore oldest groups of Neo-Hittite sculptures; Arslantepe at Malatya, where a Hittite principality is discovered still clinging to the fringes of the Plateau. Here the evidence of pottery and other archaeological considerations have led Akurgal to suggest the mid-eleventh century as an upper date for the oldest carvings.

A monumental gateway excavated by French archaeologists at Malatya has now been reconstructed in the Ankara Museum, showing its walls of 'half-timber' construction and a fine pair of guardian lions. The reliefs, carved on the face of structural masonry, are unusually small – hardly two feet high – but they occupy a prominent position, level with the tops of the lions. The scenes are of special interest. The Hittite Weather-God rides in a chariot drawn by two bulls: he descends from this chariot and receives a libation from a king, identified hieroglyphically by the name, Sulumeli. In another relief he is seen, in the presence of his son, slaying Illuyanka, the great serpent of Hittite mythology, and his attributes appear in the form of curious homunculi who reach downwards among the symbols of falling rain. There is little in these pictures for which one would not expect to find parallels in the Yazilikaya reliefs. Gods and humans are conventionally dressed and equipped and their ritual gestures are Hittite. The only innovation is a horse-drawn

Ill. 102

Ill. 103

Ill. 104

102 Sculptured portal figure from the so-called Lion Gate at Malatya. This is one of the oldest Neo-Hittite sculptures, thought to date from the mid-eleventh century BC

chariot in a lion-hunting scene, which may seem to anticipate Assyrian influence and is certainly later.

Ill. 105

Later again, perhaps by several centuries, than the Weather-God reliefs at Malatya is the colossal statue of a king which once stood in the forecourt of the gateway. Almost ten feet high and cut from a single block of stone, this figure as restored stands upright in approximately its intended position: but the circumstances in which it was found were most curious. Its base still stood before a niche in the north wall, but from this it had fallen face-downwards on the stone pavement, losing in the process its projecting right arm and damaging its face. Some time later it had been rolled into a more decorous position on its back, and a stone sarcophagus had been built around it as though it lay in a tomb. Stylistically it belongs to Akurgal's second Assyrian phase, when both ceremonial dress and coiffure had been adapted to Assyrian fashions.

Ill. 106

Styles of representation in the portrayal of hair and beard are important indications of the transition from the first to the second Assyrian style. Characteristic of the

103–105 Relief sculptures from the Lion Gate at Malatya (ancient Milid). *Above*, the Weather God arriving in his chariot and receiving a libation from a king. *Centre*, a local ruler called Sulumeli, assisted by his son, slaying a dragon known by the name Illuyanka. A third relief (*below*) shows a lion-hunting scene and is certainly of a later date. Being small in scale, these reliefs were not, as was usual with orthostats, placed against the base of the walls, but were built into them at higher level

106 Colossal statue of a king from the Lion Gate at Malatya. There are stylistic indications that this sculpture should be dated a good deal later than the relief slabs built into the walls. It would appear to represent the 'second Assyrian style', popular in the second half of the eighth century

first is a pattern consisting of separate but identical locks, each one terminating in a voluted curl. In the second the head is covered with a flat arrangement of concentric curls, terminating in a projecting cluster at the nape of the neck. Other features of Assyrian art which are prominent in both phases include particularly the appearance of chariots and horses; but there is also a great transformation in dress and weapons. The long Assyrian tunic with a tasselled sash and the fringed shawl have now replaced the short Hittite tunic and cloak. The long Assyrian sword, carried on a sling, takes the place of the shorter Hittite weapon with its crescent-shaped pommel. Shoes too have changed and the upturned toes, so characteristically Hittite, are now only worn by men of low rank, as they are today by some Anatolian peasants. Akurgal considers the first phase to begin in the mid-ninth century, when the effects of Ashurnasirpal's conquests were first felt, and the second to coincide with Tiglath-pileser III and Sargon II in the second half of the eighth century.

Ill. 107
Ill. 108

107 Relief from Carchemish showing the standing figure of King Katuwas. The arrangement of the hair suggests the so-called 'first Assyrian style'

108 Another relief from Carchemish showing ▷ a procession of officers. The hair-style here has changed, and the clustering concentric curls represent the 'second Assyrian style'

Finally then we must note the signs which are evident throughout the whole of this period, that distinctive forms of Aramaean art have been developing in those cities which have a preponderantly 'North Semitic' population. They become increasingly noticeable during the second half of the eighth century BC, when the 'traditional' Hittite style seems to be on the wane, but they may already be seen a little earlier at Sinjerli during the reign of a purely Aramaean ruler like Barrekup. His portrait, which we have already mentioned, is identified by an Aramaic inscription, and, in contrast to the Assyrian throne on which he sits, his headdress, hair and clothing show Aramaean modifications. One exclusively Aramaean practice was the erection of a sculptured stela over a tomb, and of these at least two notable examples survive, both showing unmistakably Aramaean characteristics. On one the gown of an Aramaean princess is secured by a metal clasp which conveniently dates the work to the very end of the period. It is a fibula of a Phrygian type

Ill. 98

which is plentifully represented in finds from the Great
Tumulus at Gordion, and it is also worn by the king
called Warpalawas (Urpalla) in the famous rock-relief at
Ivriz on the south-eastern edge of the Plateau. Surmount-
ing a spring, from which a huge volume of clear water
issues to irrigate an oasis of fields and fruit-gardens, the
king in this carving pays homage to a god of fertility. The
dress and hair-style of the two figures now combine
elements of all three styles – Hittite, Assyrian and
Aramaean.

It remains only to refer again to the reliefs in the gateway at Karatepe. Here, a fourth stylistic influence is evident, in elements of Egyptian art of the sort which have
reached their final decadence after adaptation and trans-
mission by Phoenician craftsmen. The resulting variety of
subjects and their haphazard juxtaposition might well,
one would think, have intimidated the most dedicated
art-historian; but they have in fact already been the
subject of much painstaking and effective study.

Ill. 143

Ills. 81, 82

Ill. 83

Ills. 85, 86

Urartu

Ill. 109

Ill. 110

The land of Urartu first appears under the name Uru-artri in Assyrian inscriptions of the thirteenth century BC. By the ninth century it is inhabited by a tribal federation of Hurrian extraction united under a 'king' called Arame, and his defeat by Shalmaneser III is one of the scenes depicted on the famous Bronze Gates of Balawat in the British Museum. After this a new Urartian dynasty was founded and the kingdom was extended by conquest to include provinces as far afield as Erzincan in the north-west, Erivan which is now in Russian Armenia, and in the south the Rowanduz area of Kurdistan. It was now permanently centred in Van, and in approximately 850 BC a king called Sarduri I made his main stronghold on the citadel rock there overlooking the lake. Into this inner homeland surrounded by high mountains, the Assyrians seemed unable to penetrate, and during the century which followed the Urartians were able further to extend their territory to Lake Urmia in the east, and in the west even as far as North Syria, thus interrupting the main trade-routes of the Assyrian empire. The first Assyrian king to deal effectively with this threat of encirclement was Tiglath-pileser III (747–727 BC) who drove the Urartians out of Syria and even made an unsuccessful attack on Van itself. Then, in 713 BC, came

109 One of the scenes depicted on the famous bronze gates from Balawat; Shalmaneser III of Assyria conducting a campaign against the tribal federation in the neighbourhood of Lake Van which subsequently became the state of Urartu. In the lower register his troops attack a city in the mountains

Sargon II's famous eighth campaign, in which he sacked their southern provincial capital, Muṣaṣir, and annexed the Urmia area. Early in the seventh century, the Urartians also began to be threatened by enemies from the north – Cimmerians first and then Scythians – and under Rusa II came another defeat by the Assyrians. From then onwards, in much reduced circumstances, the state survived in treaty relations with Assyria, until the destruction of Nineveh by the Scythians and Medes in 612 BC, soon after which it was incorporated in the empire of Cyaxares. Historically the Urartians then disappear and are replaced geographically by the Armenians, an Indo-European people of whose extraction there is no positive record.

Throughout the eastern provinces of modern Turkey, the ruined cities of Urartu are everywhere to be seen, their fortress walls often visible above ground. Built usually on a strategic hilltop or mountainside, with a strong citadel at the summit and a residential walled city on the slopes beneath, they give an interesting clue to the Urartian character. One notices the mountaineer's preference for high places, the ponderous monumentality of their architecture, remarkable feats of engineering and preoccupation with military security. With gold, silver and copper mines available in the area, Urartian art and

110 The great citadel rock at Van, overlooking the lake of that name which, under the name of Tuspa, became the first stronghold and capital of the Urartian state. Carved in cuneiform script on the face of the rock are inscriptions of the Urartian kings, some of whom were also buried here in rock-cut tombs. In the foreground are ruins of the old Turkish city

craftsmanship, particularly in the realm of metal-work, attained as we now know a high standard of excellence. Much influenced at first by the more ancient tradition of Assyria, it later acquired strongly individual characteristics which are of great interest.

Ills. 112–115

The first, ill-directed excavation of an Urartian site was made in the last century at the instigation of Sir Henry Layard. On the shoulder of rock called Toprakkale, overlooking the city of Van, the ruins of a temple dedicated to the god Haldis were ransacked and the rich contents of the building carelessly distributed to museums abroad. They consisted mostly of elaborately decorated furniture and ornamental objects of bronze or ivory. In recent years it has proved possible to reassemble some of these diagrammatically in their original relationship; and there emerges a magnificent royal throne with its matching footstool, similar to those depicted in Assyrian reliefs.

Ill. 111

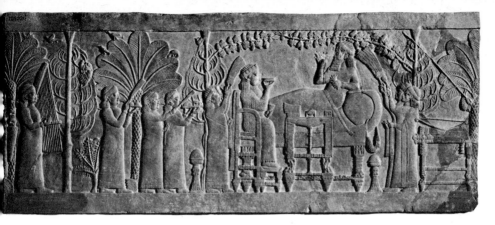

111–115 Examples of Urartian craftsmanship in metal, found
during the excavation of the Toprakkale citadel at Van. *Centre*,
a gold medallion and silver pectoral, both ornamented in *repoussé*:
below, *right*, bull's head ornament from the rim of a bronze cauldron,
and *left*, an ornamental figure in bronze, with chases for inlay,
probably part of a decorated throne. At the top is an Assyrian
relief of a feast scene in which Ashurbanipal's wife is seated upon
a throne of the type which was recovered in fragments from the
Toprakkale excavations

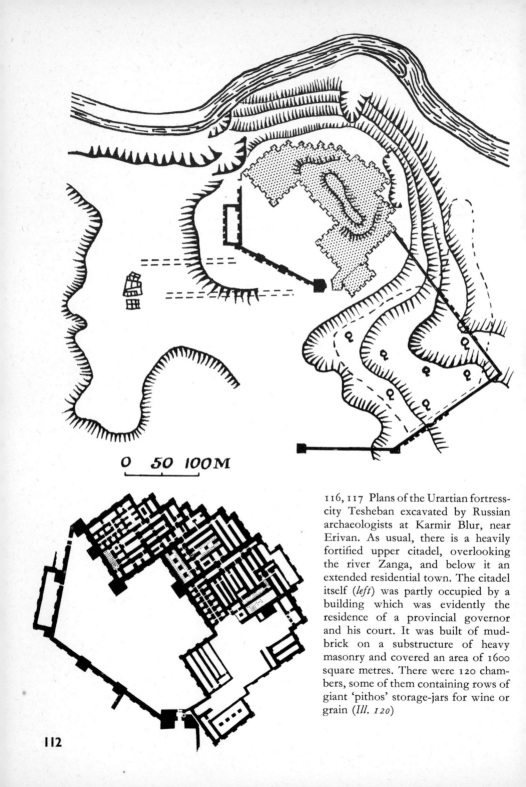

116, 117 Plans of the Urartian fortress-city Tesheban excavated by Russian archaeologists at Karmir Blur, near Erivan. As usual, there is a heavily fortified upper citadel, overlooking the river Zanga, and below it an extended residential town. The citadel itself (*left*) was partly occupied by a building which was evidently the residence of a provincial governor and his court. It was built of mud-brick on a substructure of heavy masonry and covered an area of 1600 square metres. There were 120 chambers, some of them containing rows of giant 'pithos' storage-jars for wine or grain (*Ill. 120*)

0   50   100 M

118, 119 Model in bronze from Toprakkale of a fortified building similar to that excavated at Karmir Blur. This object has been of great assistance to archaeologists in reconstructing the façade of such a building, with its projecting towers and ornamental parapet. Another fragment from the same source completes the silhouette of the tower

The first scientific excavation of an Urartian fortress-city was undertaken from 1936 onwards by Russian archaeologists at a site called Karmir Blur, overlooking the river Zanga near Erivan in Russian Armenia. The results, of which no report became available in English until 1953, were extraordinarily illuminating. Karmir Blur proved to be the site of a large and entirely characteristic provincial capital, dating mostly from the reign of Rusa II, son of Argishti II, in the first half of the seventh century B C. Of the heavily fortified citadel, about half was occupied by the palace of a provincial governor, a building covering 1600 square metres and containing 120 rooms, while on the slopes of the hill behind, there was also a residential quarter, where the houses were grouped in 'insulae' and disposed along parallel streets. The citadel walls, twelve feet thick, were built of large mud bricks on a substructure of huge undressed stones. Roofs were flat and supported on beams of pine, poplar,

Ills. 116, 133

Ills. 117, 138

120 Giant 'pithoi' in a storage chamber at Karmir Blur. These vessels were usually marked on the rim with the nature and quality of their contents. Sometimes a flooring of wooden planks was laid level with their mouths in order to give easier access to them when in use

oak and beech. The rooms were lighted both by windows high up in the walls and here and there by light-wells. Their outer façades were 'staggered' at regular intervals and provided with projecting towers, which must have accentuated their apparent height. They are also known to have terminated in crenellations whose appearance can best be judged from a fragmentary bronze model of just such a building which was among the finds made at Toprakkale. Some of the largest rooms contained rows of giant 'pithos' jars, about seven feet high, partly buried in the ground. One room, whose walls were covered with mural paintings, contained eighty-two 'pithoi', all marked on the rim with measures of capacity written either in Urartian hieroglyphs or in cuneiform. The majority were intended for wine, but one contained ninety-six bronze cups, variously inscribed with the names of kings, Menua, Argishti, Rusa and Sarduri. A huge collection of objects was recovered from this and other parts of the building.

Ills. 118, 119

Ill. 120

Ill. 121

121 From among the finds in the citadel at Karmir Blur; a simple bronze bowl bearing an inscription. Mesopotamian cuneiform was ordinarily used as a vehicle for the Urartian language, but for certain purposes, notably the inscriptions on storage vessels, a form of pictographs had come to be used, and these are not yet satisfactorily understood, though the meanings of some of them are obvious

Included among them were innumerable weapons of bronze and iron; swords, daggers, spears, quivers, arrowheads, including some of a Scythian type, a magnificent bronze helmet decorated with lion-headed serpents and *Ills. 122, 123* two rows of human or animal figures modelled in repoussé, quantities of bronze ornaments from furniture and jewellery, including gold earrings with granulated decoration. The Karmir Blur reports at last provided a sound basis for a study of Urartian archaeology.

Meanwhile, within the inner territory of Urartu which forms part of Anatolia, Turkish archaeologists had begun to contribute their own discoveries. Thanks to their researches in recent years, two sites in particular have revealed aspects of Urartian city life of which the Russian excavations had left us in ignorance. The first of these was Altintepe, near Erzincan, evidently the administrative centre of a north-westerly Urartian province. Here, in the flank of a natural hilltop, peasants discovered a

122, 123 Bronze helmets (*above*) derived from the excavations of the citadel at Karmir Blur, finely decorated with *repoussé* designs. For comparison (*below*) a fifth helmet of the same type, in the British Museum, possibly from excavations at Van itself. Soldiers wearing such helmets may be frequently seen in the Assyrian reliefs (*Ill. 130*)

stone-built tomb, and from it, among other objects, there emerged a magnificent bronze cauldron, decorated around the rim with four bulls' heads and mounted on an iron tripod. This class of object now appears to have been a characteristically Urartian device, though afterwards widely distributed in countries further west. As we shall presently see, fine examples, in which the bull protomes are replaced by human figures, were subsequently found in tumulus graves at Gordion and seem even to have penetrated as far as Greece and Etruria. At Altintepe, the full-scale excavation which followed has proved to be one of the most rewarding of our time. Confined at first to the scene of the original discovery, several more tombs were found, one of them still sealed and undisturbed. Placed at the base of a deep cutting in the slope of the citadel hill and subsequently covered with rubble, they were constructed of neat ashlar masonry with slab-vaulted roofs. There were usually three compartments:

124, 125 From an Urartian tomb at Altintepe (*right*) a bronze cauldron decorated with bull's-head protomes, standing on an iron tripod. Sometimes human heads were substituted for those of animals, as these from widely separated sites in Anatolia and the Mediterranean (*left*)

one a vestibule, another a place for offerings and a third and largest the actual tomb-chamber itself. Sometimes the burials were in stone sarcophagi, at others the bodies were laid directly upon the pavement. All round the walls were square-headed niches, similar to those found in rock-cut tombs of the Urartian period at Van and elsewhere. In the undisturbed tomb, two sarcophagi contained respectively the bodies of a man and a woman. The woman had been buried fully dressed, wearing gold buttons and a necklace of gold and semi-precious stones. With her also in the tomb were a vase of Assyrian faience, other pottery, metal trinkets and a bronze stool. All three chambers were filled with similar objects, disposed in an orderly manner on the floor; wooden furniture strengthened and embellished with ornamental bronze-work; weapons, mostly of iron, including battle-axes, arrows, lance-heads, daggers, knives and three-pronged forks. Equally important finds in the outer chamber consisted

Ill. 126

Ill. 128

126–128 Masonry-built tombs (*above* and *below*) built in the flank of the acropolis hill at Altintepe, near Erzincan. *Below*, a covered stone sarcophagus is seen and wall-niches for offerings. The tombs are vaulted with stone slabs, and usually comprise several chambers for offerings, as well as the actual burial chambers. The grave-goods were extremely rich in metal-work. A winged horse (*left*) engraved on a bronze belt recalls the classical figure of Pegasus

of horse- and war-chariot trappings, all elaborately decorated in bronze. Something of their original appearance may be gathered from the repoussé ornament on a bronze belt, on which processions of Urartian horsemen appear amongst mythical animals. Finally, cuneiform inscriptions on some of the bronzes show that the prince buried in this tomb was a contemporary of Argishti II, son of Rusa I, who reigned between 713 and 679 BC.

Ill. 127

At Altintepe, the hilltop acropolis itself proved no less interesting than the tombs. Here for the first time the well-preserved ruins of an Urartian temple were found, to clarify the equivocal evidence from Toprakkale. Further examples have more recently come to light, occupying similarly prominent positions in Urartian citadels at other sites such as Anzavur (Patnos), Cavuş Tepe near Van and Kayalidere in the Muş area, all bearing so close a resemblance to that at Altintepe that the architectural convention for religious buildings at this time can now be more perfectly understood. The plan is square, with wide but shallow buttresses at each of the four corners. Inside the sanctuary consists of a single square compartment, hardly wider than the thickness of the immensely heavy walls which surround it. These latter are built to about a man's height in neatly cut ashlar masonry, sometimes with a dedication incised in cuneiform in conspicuous positions and, above this, they can be seen to have been carried up to a considerable height in sun-dried brickwork. There is a single entrance on one side with recessed jambs, sometimes an altar facing it against the back wall of the sanctuary and some sort of built-up offering table or stela-base outside. At Altintepe the building is surrounded by a paved court, and a line of stone column bases surrounding the building in the centre of this suggests that part at least of it was roofed in. The walls of the sanctuary show signs of mural painting.

129 Fragment of a mural painting from an Urartian public building at Altintepe. This figure is one of two genii standing on either side of a sacred tree; a familiar convention in Assyrian art. They carry a situla (bucket) in one hand and hold up a pine-cone in the other. This figure is female and wears a horned 'polos'

Ill. 130

Ill. 132

There is one single instance among Assyrian records where the façade of an Urartian temple is depicted in a sculptured relief. This is the temple at Muṣaṣir, which was sacked by King Sargon II. The most notable fact about this picture, discovered in Sargon's palace at Khorsabad, is that the building is covered with a gabled roof. The low and squat proportion of the façade, as shown, could well be due to the restriction of space imposed on the sculptor. For, when looking at the plans of such buildings which have now been recovered, no architect would for a moment doubt that they suggest a tower-like structure of considerable height. Nor need one look far to find a form of monument combining these two features (a tower-like structure with a gabled roof). Remembered and imitated in a slightly later historical setting, the sixth-century 'Tomb of Cyrus' at Pasargadae provides a good example.

Also appearing to foreshadow some features of Achaemenid architecture, a second public building was found at Altintepe. This was a plain rectangular assembly-hall some forty-five metres in length, its roof supported on eighteen wooden columns arranged in three rows. Finally it should be mentioned that several other features of the Muṣaṣir relief can now be explained in terms of

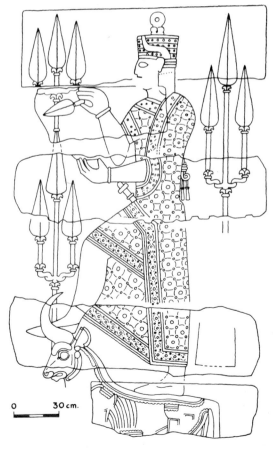

130, 131 *Above*, an Assyrian relief from Khorsabad shows King Sargon II's troops sacking the Urartian temple at Muṣaṣir. Among the ornaments of the temple one sees cauldrons on tripods (*Ill. 125*), ornamental spears and shields used as wall ornament, all of which have been found at Urartian sites. The representation of a gabled or pitched roof is a feature alien to Assyrian architecture and must be considered characteristically Urartian. *Right*, the reconstruction of an Urartian relief carving from Adilcevaz, near Lake Van, perhaps depicting the god Haldis standing on an appropriate animal. The ornamental spearheads of the Muṣaṣir relief here appear again

0   30 cm.

132 The masonry substructure of another Urartian temple at Arin Berd, also near Erivan in Russian Armenia. Like all temples of this type, its interior had been elaborately decorated with brightly coloured mural ornament

archaeological finds. Circular shields decorating the walls, symbolical spears of great size beside the doorway, and at the apex of the gable, twin vessels on tripods at the approach – identical objects to all these have now been brought to light by actual excavations which have also yielded the first examples of Urartian mural paintings and sculptured reliefs, clearly distinguishable both in style and subject-matter from those of Assyria.

Ill. 129
Ill. 131

Today then, it has come to be realized that the high accomplishment and far-reaching significance of Urartian culture has in the past been consistently underrated, simply because its remains have been insufficiently explored. Urartu is now being presented to us as a nation – and in its time a very great nation – whose history and even identity seem to have been completely expunged from the records of human memory for two-and-a-half thousand years. Yet today, everything about it – its racial characteristics, political and economic history and its art – constitute one of the most intriguing problems in Near Eastern archaeology.

133, 134 *Above*, a distant view of the citadel mound at Karmir Blur seen from the east. *Below*, the surviving ruins of the great hall in the citadel, with masonry piers which supported the roof (*cf. Ills 116, 117*)

CHAPTER SIX

The Phrygians

In the Assyrian annals one finds that, in addition to the Urartian kings, enemies in the north against whom Sargon II's campaigns were directed included the name of a ruler called 'Mita of Mushki', which is today equated with Midas of Phrygia. In the eighth century BC, the Phrygian kingdom comprised practically the whole of central and west Anatolia, from Taurus and the Urartian frontier in the east to Sardis and the Lydian hinterland of the Aegean cities. Historically, the period of several centuries during which Phrygian rule over this area had been maintained, represents an historical interlude about which, until recently, comparatively little has been known. Today, mainly as a result of excavations at the capital city of Gordion and elsewhere new interest has been aroused in the character of Phrygian culture and its possible contribution to early Greek civilization. Before excavations began, the available archaeological evidence was confined to the surviving 'Phrygian monuments': a group of rock-hewn sculptures, remotely situated in the hills to the south-east of modern Eskişehir. Identified by their discoverers in the last century as royal tombs, it has more recently been observed that each is situated near a plentiful spring or other source of fresh water and most scholars now prefer to associate them with an appropriate religious cult. In several instances, their major interest lies in the indication which they provide regarding the character of Phrygian architecture. The most striking example in this respect is the monument traditionally known as the 'Tomb of Midas' at Yazilikaya. Here the vertical rock-face is sculptured to represent the end façade of a gabled building, decorated with geometrical ornament in relief to represent terracotta tiles and crowned with a very classical-looking acroterion.

Such tantalizing glimpses of Phrygian architectural practice have been supplemented and also verified by the results of excavation. Sometimes an investigation, directed primarily towards Hittite horizons, found traces of a subsequent occupation in Phrygian times. This happened for instance at Alishar, where the highest part of the old Bronze Age citadel had been walled and fortified by some Phrygian prince. At Boghazköy (Hattušaš), the Büyükkale acropolis had been re-walled in Phrygian times. Other sites, such as Pazarli, seem to have gained in importance under the Phrygian régime; and from all of them came new evidence of material culture to supplement that from the rock-cut monuments; from Büyükkale strange outlandish sculpture; from Pazarli, striking architectural ornaments with relief designs in glazed *Ills. 136, 137* terracotta, and from everywhere characteristic Phrygian pottery, much of it finely painted. However, an adequate *Ill. 135* revelation of metropolitan life under the Phrygian rulers had to await the full-scale excavation of Gordion begun by American archaeologists in 1950.

The Phrygian capital is today represented by an enormous mound overlooking the Sangarius (Sakarya) river at a point where it is crossed by a famous highway; the Royal Road of Achaemenian Persian times. The excavators divided their attention between the mound itself and the *Ill. 138* numerous burial tumuli, dating from Phrygian and later periods, which surrounded it. Deep soundings in the

mound showed it to have been occupied at least as early
as the third millennium BC and in the later Bronze Age
to have been an important outpost of the Hittite Kingdom. Clearly it had reached a state of maximum prosperity
under the Phrygian rulers, during a period in the eighth
century which terminated in the destruction of their
kingdom by Cimmerian invaders. An impressive picture
of the city's aspect and character during this period has
been revealed by the excavations. After the preliminary
clearance of Hellenistic and Achaemenian remains beneath
Ill. 139   the summit, a Phrygian gateway of magnificent pro-
portions came to light, deeply recessed in the city walls
and strategically protected by flanking bastions of stone.

Furthermore as digging progressed inside the city,
three important public buildings were exposed, providing
in themselves the answers to many long-standing ques-
tions regarding Phrygian architecture. All three conformed to the so-called 'megaron' plan, now thought to
be of Anatolian origin, since it occurs in the Early Bronze
Age settlements at Troy and elsewhere. Each consisted
of a rectangular hall reached through a part-open portico,
one and sometimes both being provided with a huge
central hearth. Traditionally also, the walls consisted of
mud brick or stone, reinforced with a framework of

135 Graceful polychrome pottery, characteristic of the Phrygian period, buried with a young child in one of the smaller tumuli at Gordion

136, 137 Terracotta panels with reliefs decorated in coloured glaze from the Phrygian city at Pazarli in central Anatolia. *Right*, a heraldic design of opposed animals. *Below*, warrior figures which already anticipate the conventions of Greek art

138 A section of the Royal Road of the Achaemenid Persian emperors, leading from Susa in southern Iran to the Lydian capital at Sardis. This excavation was made at Gordion where the road crosses over the Sangarius (Sakarya) river

Ill. 141

Ill. 140

timber posts and crossbeams. Unparalleled however, at this period was the pavement of one hall, which consisted of a mosaic of coloured pebbles, laid in geometrical patterns. Being the earliest examples of this technique yet discovered, it is understandable that the patterns used can be seen to retain a memory of textile ornament. Equally interesting were the indications that this type of building had been covered with a gabled roof, such as is suggested by the 'Midas' monument. Two pieces of evidence seemed to point emphatically to this conclusion. The first were graffiti idly scratched on the plaster surface of the walls, among which gabled buildings were twice represented. The second was the discovery among the debris of an acroterion or finial ornament for a gable, similar to those seen crowning the rock-carved façades of the Phrygian monuments. In the third and largest megaron, it could indeed be understood that the span between walls was too great for such a roof to be constructed without intermediate support. For this purpose

139, 140 Excavations in the Phrygian city at Gordion. *Right*, a broad gateway in the main city-wall, flanked by heavy stone bastions. *Below*, inside the town, a building of the eighth century BC, its walls reinforced with a framework of timber. The pavement with its intricate design composed of coloured pebbles is probably the earliest example of mosaic work yet found

two rows of stout wooden posts had been provided, incidentally helping to support a wooden gallery running round three sides of the hall. Charred remnants of these upper structures overlaid the pavement, and crushed beneath them were found pathetic remnants of furniture, elaborately ornamented with coloured inlays or decorated with carved ivory plaques. Any disappointment felt in this respect was relieved by the rich discoveries simultaneously made in the contemporary tumuli outside the city.

The Phrygian method of burial for important personages consisted in building a tomb-chamber of timber to contain the body and grave-offerings. This was afterwards roofed in and covered by an artificial mound of earth, to protect the burial and to create a conspicuous monument. Of the three tumuli excavated by the American expedition, one at least (Tumulus P), was of moderate size and thought from the nature of its contents to have been the

grave of a young princess. The largest was that traditionally known as the 'Tomb of Midas', a colossal mound of earth, today still more than 170 feet high, creating a formidable landmark in the Sakarya valley. In this case the

excavators located the position of the actual chamber by drilling vertically from above, and then drove a tunnel towards it at plain level. The chamber, however, was covered by an inner mound of stone rubble, held in place by a retaining wall, and when this was breached, the greater part of the rubble had to be drawn off leaving a huge empty dome, with little to support the great weight of the earth above. It was therefore with some trepidation that an opening was eventually cut in the wall of the chamber itself. Nor was the internal appearance of the structure particularly reassuring. The baulks of juniper, two feet square in section, from which it was built had suffered comparatively little decay: nevertheless the roof had partially collapsed and required temporary support before the contents of the chamber could be investigated.

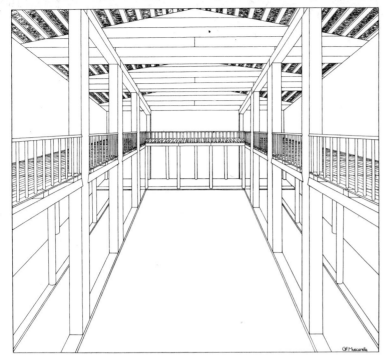

141, 142 Structural details of Phrygian architecture at Gordion. *Above*, the arrangement of upright posts and galleries in a 'megaron'-type building, probably a palace. *Below*, construction of the burial-chamber beneath the great tumulus known as the Tomb of Midas

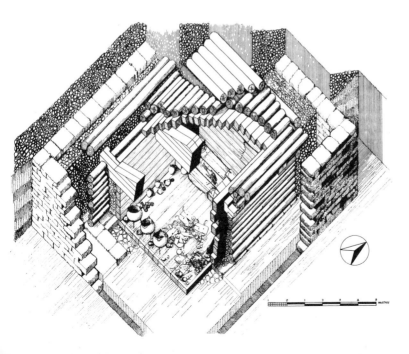

Meanwhile, the roof itself was of some interest, since it was supported by three triangular 'principals', solidly built of timber, to create the impression of a gabled building. Here was further proof that the pitched roof was a primary convention of Phrygian architecture.

As for the contents of the tomb, they proved to be sensational enough. Directly beneath the opening, the skeleton of a Phrygian king lay upon a huge collapsed bed among the decaying remains of no less than twenty rich coverlets. Behind, against the farther wall, were the remains of elaborate furniture, inlaid with rare woods in intricate patterns. One piece had consisted of shelves on which rested many scores of bronze vessels. Its collapse spilled out a cascade of metal over the floor, where it now lay filling the whole chamber with the brilliant peacock blue of patinated bronze. Against the side walls stood gigantic copper cauldrons on iron tripods, which had contained food and drink; these were ornamented at their rims with *Ill. 124* the busts of bearded men or with female figures of the type known later in Greece as 'sirens'. Strange devices of embossed leather which had decorated the walls also covered the floor. Some of the bronze vessels bore *Ill. 145* inscriptions incised in wax, which should help to throw new light on a Phrygian script today still imperfectly understood. But the most puzzling aspect of this tomb, in view of the Midas legend, was the total absence of gold and silver or weapons enriched with precious stones. The only personal ornaments with which the king was provided consisted of more than seventy bronze 'safety-pins' (fibulae) contained in a linen bag.

Regarding the approximate date of these three Phrygian burials, it was first assumed that they must have been made previously to the disaster associated with the arrival of the Cimmerians, which took place in about 680 BC. Stylistically there was nothing among their contents which would be inconsistent with a date late in the

143 An ornamental fibula or safety-pin from the great tumulus at Gordion. An identical ornament is worn by King Warpalawas in the Ivriz relief (*Ill. 82*)

eighth century BC. This assumption was satisfactorily confirmed when a closer study of the grave-goods had been made. A bucket-shaped vessel (situla) decorated with a lion's head is exactly depicted in a relief from the palace of King Sargon II of Assyria (721–705 BC). A fluted bowl, moulded from colourless glass which was discovered in the child's tomb, elsewhere finds a precise parallel in a glass jar inscribed in cuneiform with the name of the same king. One of the studded bronze fibulae found in the Great Tumulus is identical to that worn by King Warpalawas of Tyana at Ivriz. Warpalawas is known to have become a vassal of Assyria in 738 BC.

Five vessels of various shapes from the Great Tumulus at Gordion bear short inscriptions in an alphabetical script which at present cannot be read. Nevertheless, some significance may be attached to the fact that three of the five are inscribed on smears of wax overlaid on the bronze. Ever since the discovery at Assyrian Nimrud, in a comparably dated setting, of cuneiform inscriptions in a 'book' whose 'pages' were prepared with wax, the possibility of a preference in ancient Anatolia for this system of writing has been much discussed. It would explain for instance the puzzling non-survival of written records in the administrative centres of West Anatolian states from the Middle Bronze Age onwards. As for the Phrygian script itself, it must be remembered that the earliest Greek alphabetical script was at this period already in use in the Aegean cities, and it was for long assumed that the Phrygian system of writing must have been adapted directly from this fairly accessible source. Against this it has been argued that between Phrygia and the coast lay the country of Lydia with a peculiar alphabet of its own, and it has been alternatively suggested that both scripts, Phrygian and Greek, have a common origin elsewhere. North Syria is known to have been the area from which the Phoenician alphabet was transmitted to

Ill. 146
Ill. 144

Ill. 143

Ills. 81, 82

Ill. 145

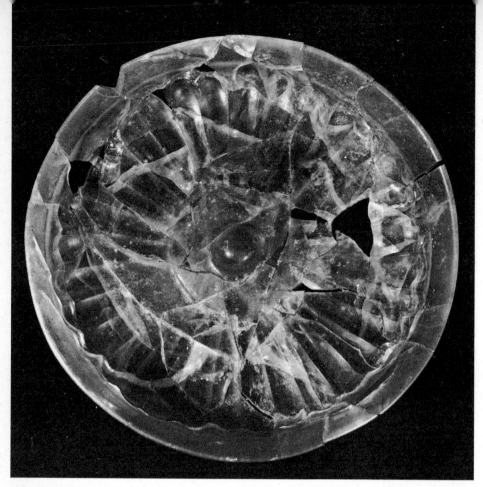

144, 145 Treasures from the Phrygian tumulus burials at Gordion. *Above*, a bowl of colourless glass with moulded ornament, a material extremely rare in the eighth century BC when rock-crystal was more common. *Below*, a bronze bowl bearing a Phrygian inscription engraved on a tiny panel of wax near the rim

146 Found in the great tumulus at Gordion, a bronze situla or ceremonial bucket in the shape of a lion's head. Identical vessels are carried by acolytes appearing in procession on Assyrian reliefs of the eighth century BC

the Greeks and it was there perhaps that both Greeks and Phrygians simultaneously adapted the North Semitic writing to their use by introducing vowels. By the great eastern trade-route upon which it lies, Gordion is no further from the Orontes than Greece.

Apart from alphabetical affinities and a preference for gabled buildings, other equally significant aspects of Phrygian culture suggest a relationship with contemporary Greece. There is already something European in the background of Phrygian art, and when, after the Cimmerian invasion in 680 BC, the Midas dynasty came to an end and its dominion was usurped by a Lydian kingdom with its capital at Sardis, Anatolian culture seemed to lose much of its individual character and to assimilate itself to that of the now flourishing cities on the Aegean coast. The timeless tradition of regionally characteristic thought and behaviour, the seeds of which had been sown in remote prehistoric times, had now run its full course. The peninsula had become no more than a bridge between east and west.

Bibliography

AKURGAL, E. *Art of the Hittites*, London, 1962
— *Phrygische Kunst*, Ankara, 1955
ARIK, R.O. *Les Fouilles d'Alaca Höyük*, Ankara, 1937
BITTEL, K. *Grundzüge zur Vorgeschichte Kleinasiens*, 2nd ed., Tübingen, 1950
BLEGEN, C.W. *et. al. Troy*, 4 vols. Princeton, 1950, 1951, 1953, 1958
BOSSERT, H. *Altanatolien*, Berlin, 1942 (Picture album)
CAMBRIDGE ANCIENT HISTORY FASCICLES
  BLEGEN, C.W. 'Troy', vol. I, ch. XVIII; XXIV; vol. II, ch. XV; XXI
  GURNEY, O.R. 'Anatolia *c.* 1750–1600 BC': 'Anatolia *c.* 1600–1380 BC', vol. II, ch. VI; XVa
  LEWY, H. 'Anatolia in the Old Assyrian Tablets', vol. I, ch. XXIV, 7–10
  MELLAART, J. 'Anatolia before *c.* 4000 BC': 'Anatolia *c.* 2300–1750 BC', vol. I, ch. VII,
    11–14; XXIV, 1–6
  —'Anatolia *c.* 4000–2300 BC', vol. I, ch. XVIII
FISCHER, P. *Bogazköy, Die Hethitische Keramik*, Berlin, 1963
GARELLI, P. *Les Assyriens en Cappadoce*, Paris, 1963
GARSTANG, J. *Prehistoric Mersin*, Oxford, 1953
GARSTANG, J. and GURNEY, O.R. *The Geography of the Hittite Empire*, British Institute of
  Archaeology at Ankara, Occas. Paper No. 5, London, 1959
GOETZE, A. 'Die Annalen des Mursilis'. *Mitteilungen der Vorderasiatisch-aegyptischen Gesellschaft*,
  38 (1933)
— *Kizzuwadna and the Problem of the Hittite Geography*, Yale, 1940.
— *Kleinasien*, 2nd ed., Munich, 1957
GOLDMAN, H. *Excavations at Gözlu Kule, Tarsus*, vols. II, III, Princeton, 1950, 1956
GURNEY, O.R. *The Hittites*, Harmondsworth, 2nd ed., 1961
GÜTERBOCK, H. 'The Deeds of Suppiluliuma as told by his son Mursili II', *Journal of Cunei-
  form Studies*, X, 1956
HUXLEY, G.L. *Achaeans and Hittites*, Oxford, 1960
KOŞAY, H.Z. *Ausgrabungen von Alaca Höyük*, Ankara, 1944
— *Les Fouilles d'Alaca Höyük*, 1937–39, Ankara, 1951
LLOYD, S. and MELLAART, J. *Beycesultan*, I and II. British Institute of Archaeology at Ankara,
  London, 1962, 1964
LLOYD, S. *Early Anatolia*, Harmondsworth, 1956
MELLAART, J. *Earliest Civilizations of the Near East*, London, 1965
MELLINK, M.J. 'Anatolia: Old and New Perspectives'. In *Proc. American Philosophical Soc.*,
  110, 2, 1966
— 'Anatolian Chronology'. In R. Ehrich, *Chronologies in Old World Archaeology*, Chicago, 1966
NAUMANN, R. *Architektur Kleinasiens*, Tubingen, 1955
ÖZGÜÇ, N. *Kültepe-Kanis*, Ankara, 1959
— *Anatolian Group of Cylinder Seal Impressions from Kültepe*, Ankara, 1965
ÖZGÜÇ, T. *Excavations at Horoztepe*, Ankara, 1958
— 'The Statuette from Horoztepe'. In *Anatolia*, III, 1958
— 'Excavations at Altintepe'. In *Belleten*, XXV, 98, April 1961
— 'Early Anatolian Archaeology in the light of Recent Researches'. In *Anatolia*, VII, 1963
— 'The Urartian Architecture on the Summit of Altintepe'. In *Anatolia*, VII, 1963
— 'The Art and Architecture of Ancient Kanish'. In *Anatolia*, VIII, 1964
— 'New Finds from Horoztepe'. In *Anatolia*, VIII, 1964
— *Altintepe*, Ankara, 1966
YOUNG, R.S. 'Gordion of the Royal Road', *Proc. American Philosophical Soc.*, 107, 4, 1963
  (see also *American Journal of Archaeology* for interim reports on excavations)

List of Illustrations

The author and publishers are grateful to the many official bodies, institutions, and individuals mentioned below for their assistance in supplying illustration material. Illustrations without acknowledgement are from originals in the archives of Thames & Hudson.

137

87 Plan of Carchemish. Drawn by Lucinda Rodd after Woolley

88 Detail of a fortress on the Balawat Gates. British Museum. Photo courtesy of the Trustees of the British Museum

89 Relief of soldiers, Carchemish. Photo courtesy of the Trustees of the British Museum

90 'Royal Buttress', Carchemish. Photo courtesy of the Trustees of the British Museum

91 'Long Wall of Sculptures', Carchemish. Photo courtesy of the Trustees of the British Museum

92 Detail of 'Long Wall of Sculptures', Carchemish. Photo courtesy of the Trustees of the British Museum

93 Relief of musicians, Carchemish. Photo courtesy of the Trustees of the British Museum

94 Seated god on lions, Carchemish. Photo courtesy of the Trustees of the British Museum

95 Seated goddess, Kubaba, Carchemish. Photo courtesy of the Trustees of the British Museum

96 Relief of priestesses, Carchemish. Photo courtesy of the Trustees of the British Museum

97 Stela of Esarhaddon of Assyria, 681-669 BC, from Sinjerli. Staatliche Museen, Berlin. Museum photo

98 Basalt statue of a god standing on lions from Sinjerli. Archaeological Museum, Istanbul

99 Relief of Barrekup from Sinjerli. Staatliche Museen, Berlin. Museum photo

100 Plan of Sinjerli. Drawn by Lucinda Rodd after Akurgal

101 Relief with Hittite hieroglyphs. Ankara Museum. Photo courtesy of Professor O. Gurney

102 Lion from gateway, Malatya. Ankara Museum

103-5 Stone reliefs from Malatya. Ankara Museum

106 Colossal statue of a king from Malatya. Ankara Museum

107 Relief of King Katuwas from Carchemish. Ankara Museum

108 Relief of officers from Carchemish. Ankara Museum. Photo Josephine Powell

109 Assyrian army defeating Urartians in 859 BC. Detail of Balawat bronze gates. British Museum. Photo courtesy of the Trustees of the British Museum

110 Van Citadel from south. Photo Josephine Powell

111 Ashurbanipal feasting. Relief from North Palace, Nineveh. British Museum. Photo courtesy of the Trustees of the British Museum

112 Gold medallion from Toprakkale. Staatliche Museen, Berlin. Museum photo

113 Silver pectoral from Toprakkale. Staatliche Museen, Berlin. Museum photo

114 Bronze throne fragment from Toprakkale. British Museum. Photo courtesy of the Trustees of the British Museum

115 Bronze bull's head protome from Toprakkale. British Museum. Photo

courtesy of the Trustees of the British Museum

116 Plan of fortress of Karmir Blur. Drawn by Stephen Molnar after Piotrovsky

117 Plan of city of Karmir Blur. Drawn by Stephen Molnar after Piotrovsky

118 Bronze model of a tower from Toprakkale. British Museum. Photo courtesy of the Trustees of the British Museum

119 Bronze plaque with relief of a citadel from Toprakkale. British Museum. Photo courtesy of the Trustees of the British Museum

120 Storerooms, Karmir Blur. Photo Professor B. B. Piotrovsky, courtesy of Dr R. D. Barnett

121 Bronze gilt dish from Karmir Blur. State Historical Museum, Moscow. Photos Professor B. B. Piotrovsky, courtesy of Professor D. M. Lang

122 Urartian helmets from Karmir Blur. State Historical Museum, Moscow. Photo Professor B. B. Piotrovsky, courtesy of Dr R. D. Barnett

123 Unprovenanced Urartian helmet. British Museum. Photo courtesy of the Trustees of the British Museum

124 Bronze human-headed cauldron protomes from Toprakkale, Olympia, Gordion and Praeneste

125 Urartian cauldron and stand from Altintepe. Ankara Museum. Photo courtesy of the Director

126 Sealed entrance to undisturbed tomb, Altintepe. Photo courtesy of Professor T. Özgüç

127 Winged horse engraved on bronze from Altintepe. Ankara Museum. Photo courtesy of Professor T. Özgüç

128 Sarcophagi in undisturbed tomb, Altintepe. Photo courtesy of Professor T. Özgüç

129 Fragment of Urartian wall painting. Photo courtesy of Professor T. Özgüç

130 Sack of the Urartian temple at Muşaşir. Relief from the Palace of Sargon at Khorsabad. After Botta

131 Reconstruction of a relief from Adilcevaz. Drawn by Lucinda Rodd after Burney and Lawson

132 Stone wall of the Urartian temple at Arim Berd. Photo courtesy of Professor Stuart Piggott

133 Karmir Blur from the east. Photo courtesy of Professor Stuart Piggott

134 Great hall, Karmir Blur. Photo Professor R. Hovannisian, courtesy of Professor D. M. Lang

135 Painted pottery from the 'Child's Tomb', Gordion. Ankara Museum. Photo Josephine Powell

136, 137 Phrygian terracotta reliefs from Pazarli. Ankara Museum. Photos Josephine Powell

138 'Royal Road', Gordion. Photo courtesy of Professor R. S. Young

139 Phrygian gateway, Gordion. Photo courtesy of Professor R. S. Young

140 Coloured pebble mosaic, Gordion. Photo courtesy of Professor R. S. Young

141 Megaron interior reconstruction, Gordion. Photo Professor R. S. Young

142 Reconstruction of the 'Tomb of Midas', Gordion. Drawn by Martin Weaver based on information supplied by Professor R. S. Young

143 Studded ornamental bronze fibula from the 'Tomb of Midas', Gordion. Photo courtesy of Professor R. S. Young

144 Glass bowl from the 'Child's Tomb', Gordion. Ankara Museum. Photo Josephine Powell

145 Bronze bowl with inscription incised in wax from Gordion. Photo courtesy of Professor R. S. Young

146 Bronze situla from the 'Tomb of Midas', Gordion. Painting by Piet de Jong, courtesy of Professor R. S. Young

Index

Numbers in italics refer to illustrations

144

DATE DUE

DEMCO 38-297